A Think Tank Education Publication 2013-2018

"For precept must be upon precept; precept upon precept; line upon line, line upon line; here a little, and there a little." Isaiah 28:10

There is a song that we sing, "Let the Beauty of Jesus Be Seen In You". The verses say this:

> "Let the beauty of Jesus be seen in me
> All His wonderful passion and purity
> May His spirit divine all my being refine
> Let the beauty of Jesus be seen in me.
>
> When somebody has been so unkind to you
> Some word spoken that pierces you through and through
> Think how He was beguiled, spat upon, and reviled
> Let the beauty of Jesus be seen in you.
>
> From the dawn of the morning to close of day
> In example, in deeds, and in all you say
> Lay your gifts at His feet, ever strive to keep sweet
> Let the beauty of Jesus be seen in you."

Written by Albert W.T. Orsborn, 1916
Verses 2 and 3 by George L Johnson, 1934
Music by Tom M. Jones, 1927

Satan, through our society, tries to show us that our beauty is something that we make happen, something in which we can take pride. As he always does, he mixes a little bit of truth with lies. We do make our beauty happen – but only when we seek to be the beauty that God would have us to be. That beauty has very little to do with our face, our clothes, and our hair. Rather, the way we wear those things REFLECTS the TRUE BEAUTY that we have within.

I hope that through this study, you can come to see the beauty that is in you already and the beauty you can grow to be in the Lord.

Blessings,
Mrs. Angela Legg

Table of Contents

Lesson One

God Delights in Each of Us

A Good Verse to Remember: Ephesians 2:10

1. Read – Jeremiah 31:3. Write this verse here:

God is talking to Judah through Jeremiah. He's telling them that He is going to keep His promise and protect a remnant of the nation He created. But we can apply this verse to us as well. Do you know why?

2. Read 1 Jn. 4:19; Ps. 103:17; 2 Thess. 2:13-16; Eph. 2:4-5

   Reading these verses together, how would you describe the love of God for us?

3. Read Matthew 10:29-31 and Luke 12:5-7.
   Who does God care for in these verses?

4. Does God value you?

5. What is "value" (how you define it AND a book definition)?

6. Does God value the sparrow more than man does?

7. Why a "sparrow"? What point is the Spirit making using this bird instead of an eagle, a lion, or an elephant?

Do you know how many hairs are on your own head? Does your mother? Isn't it amazing that the Lord KNOWS the answer to that question!

9. Read Psalms 139:13-17
   How long has God been aware of you?

10. Think of God as an artist and you as a piece of art – were you made by accident or with intent and an eye for detail?

11. When did God write about us?

12. Read Psalm 139:14
    What does David mean by "fearfully and wonderfully made"?

13. Write a short prayer praising God for His creation of you.

14. Read – Psalm 149:4
    Who does the Lord take pleasure in?

    What does "take pleasure" mean?

    For what will the Lord use salvation?

15. Read Psalm 103:13-14

    The NKJV uses the word "pities" in verse 13. Look in other translations and write down what words they use here.

    Write what this verse means in your own words.

16. How does that make you feel? Does God seem far away and uninterested in you OR does He seem to know everything about you and to be close by?

17. Read Psalm 8:3-9
    How do these verses make you feel when you read them?

Verses 4 and 5 talk about the value God has set on mankind, even though mankind has done nothing to earn it. This shows us how much God loves us. We have a purpose!

18. Write a prayer that you can say to thank God for something wonderful He has created.

19. Read Zephaniah 3:17
    What does this verse say that God will do?

Read these verses for discussion in class:

Ecclesiastes 12:13   Ephesians 1:9
Ephesians 3:11   Psalm 102:18
Acts 17:26-27

Conclusion:

Having read all these scriptures, how do you feel about yourself, looking through God's eyes?

Do you see that He created you and is aware of your needs and wants?
Do you see that He loves you very much?

God has given you value by creating you. Your being here means you have something to offer. Never let anyone, even your own self, tell you that you have nothing to offer or that you are nothing.

Final Thought: We will explore this thought more in future lessons, but we absolutely need to remember, from the beginning, that the FACT that God created us, gave us a home here, provided means for a home in heaven, and all the blessings in between means that He is due our respect and honor as the absolute authority in our life. We must not let the world distract us from that fact!

Study Builders

To help you to begin a knowledge base of verses that will help you to achieve the goal set out in 1 Timothy 4:12 (which we will look at more closely in Lesson 2); the following STUDY BUILDERS will be something that you add to each week. Every lesson will have verses that go on any, or all, four of the BUILDERS. These will help you to see that God not only tells you to do things – He SHOWS you HOW!

The STUDY BUILDERS are four sections titled as follows:

In Manner of Life/In Purity

(These two are together because it seemed redundant to separate them. If you are doing something in the way you live your life that is pleasing to God, then you are pure. If you are making pure and wholesome decisions, then this is the way you live your life. They are tied together.)

In Word

In Love

In Faith

Fill the pages with scriptures that show you how to be what God wants you to be in these areas.

This is where the lessons become YOURS. You put these thoughts and ideas into a place where you understand them best. I may think that the fruits of the Spirit from Galatians 5:22-23 go on all four sections, but you might believe they only need to go on the "In Manner of Life/In Purity" section. It's YOUR study – YOU will get out of it what YOU put into it.

Study Builders

Use this page to note all the verses from the lesson into one or more of the categories.

In Manner of Life In Purity	In Word
In Love	In Faith

Additional Notes:

Lesson 2

Respect for All Authority

We mentioned in Lesson 1 that God is our absolute authority. This means He has the right to expect and demand our obedience and respect. As the absolute authority, He has also told us to respect others in relation to us.

1. Read Genesis 1:1. Who was in the beginning?

2. Read Romans 1:16-23. What is "evident" and "clearly seen"?

   How long has it been so?

3. In Isaiah 29:15-16 Isaiah tells us about some people who have tried to hide their plans from the Lord. Explain what Isaiah says this behavior of acting as though no one is watching you is REALLY saying.

4. Psalm 90 beautifully describes just how GREAT God is. Moses wrote this Psalm. I can just see him after a rebellion of the people, thinking these things and wishing the people would just realize it.

Write Psalm 90:2 here.

How long has God been God?

How long will He continue to be God?

5. Ephesians 2:10 is the verse you memorized in the last lesson. Note the breakdown of the verse:
   a. We are His workmanship
   b. Created, in Christ Jesus, for good works
   c. These good works God prepared beforehand
   d. These good works were prepared so that we would walk in them.

We were created by Him, in the beginning. We are created AGAIN, in Christ. God IS our authority BECAUSE He made us: choosing to ignore it, like those in Romans 1:22-23, doesn't change the facts.

6. As a reminder of something I'm sure you already know, READ Matthew 8:5-13. We learn a lesson here about delegated authority. Explain what it is the Centurion understood and what Jesus said this man's understanding indicated.

God has authority. He then delegates authority. If we respect Him, we MUST respect those He put in authority over us.

7. Read John 5:25-27. Who has God given authority to execute judgment over us?

8. In Ephesians 1:18-23 Paul explains that God has put ALL things in subjection under whom?

9. Read Matthew 22:15-22 and Romans 13:1-7.
    Who is said to have authority in these two verses?

    Where does the authority originate?

10. According to Romans 13:2, who are you opposing if you resist the authority of the government?

11. Write Titus 3:1 here.

Read Ephesians 6:1-3 and Colossians 3:20.

12. What is the first commandment with promise?

13. What will obeying it do for you?

14. When did God first make this commandment?

15. What does "honor" mean?

16. Why should children obey their parents, according to Colossians 3:20?

17. Write a prayer that asks God to help you obey Him in this way.

18. Read 1 Peter 5:1-5 and Hebrews 13:17.
    What is the "job" of an Elder?

19. Read 1 Thessalonians 5:12-13
     These verses are talking about the elders of the congregation. In your own words, explain what these verses are telling us to do.

20. What does "esteem them very highly" means?

21. Draw a chart that illustrates the placement of authority from 1 Corinthians 11:3.

22. Who is subject to whom, in Ephesians 5:22, 24?

     How is she to be subject to him?

The phrase "as to the Lord" is an important qualifier. If you don't know how to do something "to the Lord" then how will you do this thing that is done in the same way?

23. Read Romans 12:10
     This chapter in Romans is telling Christians how to behave toward one another. What does this verse tell us to do?

24. Are we supposed to get what we want first, and then try to help others?

Read 1 Peter 2:13-17.
25. Whom are you to honor?

26. What are we to do towards God?

Look up in Strong's Concordance the word "fear" in this verse. Find out what the Greek definition of the original word said. Is this different than you expected or thought it meant?

27. In James 4:7 we are told to do two things. List them here.
      a.

      b.

28. Read Matthew 19:19
     There are two commandments that the rich ruler said he had always kept. What are they and can you think of an example of how to obey each one of these commands?

Read 1 Timothy 5:1-2
29. How should you speak to people older than yourself?

What does "rebuke" and "exhort" mean?

30. In verse 2, it says "younger women as sisters". Which does this mean?

   a) to treat all young women in the same way you do your siblings, like being short-tempered, bossy, and aggravated with them OR

   b) to treat young women as sisters by showing them love and respect and trying to care for them the same way you should, and hopefully do, care for your "brethren" by birth?

Conclusion:

1 Timothy 4:12 is written to Timothy who is working as a preacher. The verse can be applied to everyone, in general application, as well.

Explain what you understand "let no one despise your youth" means, in your own words. How could someone despise your youth?

List the things in which we can be examples.
1.
2.
3.
4.
5.

If you are always working to be what God wants you to be in these things, then you will always be a good example to others. Being a good example is part of building the character that makes for a good reputation. You can't always control the reputation, but you can always control your character. That being said, a good reputation is something you should always desire to have! So do what YOU can to build a good one.

In Your Bible:
Isaiah 44:2
Hebrews 13:8
Acts 4:19-20
Acts 5:29
John 5:37
John 6:57
John 12:49
1John 4:14
Ephesians 6:7
Colossians 3:23

Study Builders

Use this page to note all the verses from the lesson into one or more of the categories.

In Manner of Life In Purity	In Word

In Love	In Faith

Additional Notes:

Lesson 3

Lessons from the First Woman (Eve)

Scripture references: Genesis 1:26-4:2, 25;1 Corinthians 11:8-9, 11-12;2 Corinthians 11:3; 1 Timothy 2:13-15; 1 John 2:16

1. Read Genesis 2:20. What did God notice was missing for Adam?

NOTE: Names mean things. Whenever possible, research the names of the people you study. Often you get insight into them and why God used them.

2. Define "Adam".

3. Define "Eve".

4. How was Adam created? (Gen. 2:7)

5. How was Eve created? (Gen. 2:21-22)

6. What was Adam's response when God brought her to him? (Gen. 2:23)

7. Moses comments on the natural result of Eve being created from Adam's rib in Gen. 2:24. What does he say?

8. In a few sentences, tell the story of Eve and the serpent from Genesis 3.

9. Read 1 John 2:16. List the three things that are "all that is in the world".

   a.

   b.

   c.

10. Read Gen. 3:6. What three things does Eve recognize about the tree after the serpent encourages her to eat it?

   a.

   b.

   c.

11. Eve is mentioned in the New Testament too. Look at 1 Timothy 2:12-15 and 2 Cor. 11:3. What do we learn about Eve and what do we learn about Adam from these verses?

   a.

   b.

Because of how Eve responded to Satan's deception, God provided a means of protection for all women, IF we will use it!

12. In what way did Adam and Eve try to correct the problem of their nakedness? (Gen.3:7)

13. Their "covered" did not cover, so what did God do? (Gen. 3:21)

14. God IS fair and just. Read Genesis 3:8-19. Explain how God was merciful, fair, and just in His handling of their sin. (Remember Gen. 2:17!)

15. Notice Genesis 3:16. God tells Eve the order of things. Describe that order.

This is still God's plan today! We can read in 1 Corinthians 11:8-9, 11-12 where Paul explains authority to the church in Corinth.

16. The legacy Eve left is seen in Cain and Abel. They aren't the story here in this lesson, but let's note their connections to Eve.

   Define "Cain" and write what Eve said about him after his birth.

   Define "Abel".

   Could the meaning of his name refer to what was to come later in his life?

   Define "Seth" and write what Eve said about him after he was born.

We all lost the Garden of Eden when Adam and Eve did. Interesting thing though, we all gained something when Cain murdered Abel. Seth was born, and it is through him that CHRIST comes. God's plan is built with a way for us to get back to Eden in Heaven! A pattern begins here of God using unlikely circumstances, for example Cain's sin, to bring about His will for mankind. Keep an eye out for it as you study your Bible, it might surprise you just how often that happens!

Conclusion:

Eve was ready with her observances of the tree. Satan deceived her, but it seems that he played upon things she already had in her mind. We have to actively protect ourselves from her downfall. We also have to trust God for the order He set in place between men and women. Let's fill our minds with thankfulness and good things (Phil. 4:8) so bitterness, discontent, and jealousy can't find a way to trip us up.

In Your Bible: Colossians 2:6-7; Proverb 3:5-6

Study Builders

Use this page to note all the verses from the lesson into one or more of the categories.

In Manner of Life In Purity	In Word
In Love	In Faith

Additional Notes:

Lesson 4

Lessons from one Called "Princess" (Sarah)

Scripture References: Genesis 11-12; 16-18; 20-21; 23; 24:36; 25:10; 49:31; Rom. 9:9; Galatians 4:21-31;Hebrews 11:11-12; 1 Peter 3:5-6

Do you remember in the last lesson we talked about God using circumstances to accomplish His will? In Romans 9:3-13, Paul makes this very point. He is telling the Roman Christians that God has adopted the Gentiles along with Jews. There were teachers who were saying that only Jews could be Christians because they were descended from Abraham. Read verses 7-9. What was made that decided who the descendants of Abraham and Sarah were?

1 Cor.1:18-31 teaches about the wisdom of the world versus the wisdom of God. Over and over men think that God's way is foolishness, when it really is wise. It didn't make sense to the Jews that Gentiles could be included, because their "wisdom" wasn't spiritual – it was physical. Sarah is an example for us of God using circumstances to accomplish His will in ways that men just don't understand at first.

1. Briefly, tell the story of Sarah as read in the references listed above. What is the beginning, the middle, and the end of her story?

2. How are Abram and Sarai related? (Gen.20:12)

3. What does Abram mean?

   What does Abraham mean?

4. What does Sarai mean?

   What does Sarah mean? (Gen. 17:16)

Let's look at Genesis 12:10-20 and Genesis 20:1-18 together.

5. Why did Abraham deceive Pharaoh and Abimelech about Sarah?

6. Did hiding this information protect them both, the way Abraham intended?

7. In Gen. 12:15-20 and Gen. 20:2-7, what was God's attitude toward Pharaoh and Abimelech for marrying another man's wife?

8. Did Abraham's lie ONLY affect him?   Yes or No   If No, list everyone affected by his choice to deceive these two kings.

NOTE:

a. Each of these men took Sarah with the intent of her being his wife! Notice that GOD said that she was ABRAHAM'S wife.

b. Sarah's reputation as a "one man woman" was important! God protected her reputation, and both kings made sure there was no question she "belonged" to Abraham. (Gen. 12:20 and Gen. 20:16)

God made promises to Abram in Genesis 12 and 15. The only way these promises would come true is if Abram had a son of his own. We know from Genesis 16:1, that Sarai had not given him any children.

9. Did Sarai solve her problems by creating the circumstances for the birth of Ishmael?

10.Was she the ONLY one affected by her impatience and discontent?

11.According to Hebrews 11:11, Sarah learned her lesson and received what blessing?

12.Did God keep His promise to Abraham and Sarah? (Gen.21:2)

13.What did God tell them to name the baby? (Gen. 21:1-7)

What does his name mean?

For fun, let's do some MATH!

14. In Gen.12:4, it says that Abram was 75 years old when God told him to leave his home. In Gen. 16:16, it says that Abram was 86 years old when Ishmael was born. How many years had Abram and Sarai been waiting for a baby since being told their family would be a large one?

15. In Genesis 17:1, it says that Abraham is 99 years old. Using the information from the last question - How old is Ishmael?

16. Add Ishmael's age to the answer from #14 and give how many years Sarah and Abraham have been waiting to have a child of their own.

17. If Sarah will be 90 years old when the baby is born, a year from now, how old is Sarah now? (Gen. 17:17, 21)

18. How old was Sarah when God made the promises in Genesis 12 to Abraham? (hint, answer to #17 minus the answer to # 16 or Gen. 12:4 minus 10 years)

19. How long did Sarah wait before baby Isaac was born?

20. Did waiting for a baby lessen Sarah's joy in having Isaac?

21. Write Psalm 27:14 here.

22. Did God provide for Hagar and Ishmael? (Gen.21)

We've seen Sarah in some "questionable" moments. These are the stories God chose to share with us about her. Take a look at how God summed up her life (Heb.11:11). We are told to follow her in the things she did right.

Read 1 Peter 3:1-6.

23. In 1 Peter 3:5-6, what should we do "just as Sarah"?

24. Read 1 Peter 3:4, 5. Describe the adornment that "holy women" put on.

25. Look up "gentle" (some translations say "meek") and "quiet". Discuss HOW we CAN be these things.

Note: Remember this description – we will study it more when we study on modesty and purity in other lessons.

Conclusion:

Sarah is an example to us of many things but one of the most important is God keeping His promises. This is yet another thread that runs from Genesis through Revelation. It is brought to fruition in Christ's death and resurrection. We need to understand and KNOW this concept. GOD KEEPS HIS PROMISES. We see in Galatians 4:21-31 how God uses Sarah and Hagar to make this point, and to drive home the FREEDOM found in His promise of salvation through Jesus. In verse 23, Ishmael is said to be a son "according to the flesh" and Isaac is the son "through the promise". Hagar's children go on to remain in slavery, while Sarah's children are free. Freedom is found in doing things God's way, in His time, not our own. Bondage is the only thing found in holding to something other than God's will for us in Christ.   So CHOOSE to be a child of Sarah – the FREE woman – be dressed in subjection with a gentle and quiet spirit, and in this way begin to put on the beauty that God finds "precious"!

In Your Bible:

Psalm 4:5; Psalm 9:10; Proverb 3:5; Proverb 30:5; Isaiah 51:2

Study Builders

Use this page to note all the verses from the lesson into one or more of the categories.

In Manner of Life In Purity	In Word
In Love	In Faith

Additional Notes:

Lesson 5

Lessons from Rebekah, Rachel, and Leah; Jochebed, and Miriam

Scripture References: Gen. 22:23; Gen. 24-28; Gen. 49:31; Gen. 29-31; Gen. 33; Gen. 35; Ruth 4:11; Gen. 34:1

<u>REBEKAH</u>

1. Read Genesis 22:23. How is Rebekah related to Abraham?

2. Describe Rebekah. (Gen.24:15-16)

3. The servant is stopping Rebekah in the middle of her work – how does she respond? (Gen. 24:17-21)

4. Did Rebekah do only what she was asked by the servant?

5. Did Rebekah delay leaving because she was nervous and afraid?

6. Did Rebekah pine for home when once on the road?

7. Rebekah made more trouble for Isaac after she arrived.   Use a verse to prove your answer.   True or False   Verse _____

8. Rebekah had to wait _____ years for her children. (Gen. 25:20, 26)

9. Read Genesis 27:5-17. Rebekah had a positive influence on the relationships in her family.   True or False

10. What are some of the consequences of Rebekah and Jacob's deceptions? (Gen. 27:41-46)

11. NAMES Research

Rebekah –

Esau –

Jacob –

RACHEL AND LEAH

12. How did Rachel go about doing her duties? (Gen. 29:12)

13. Describe Rachel and Leah using Gen. 29:17. You may need to look up the Hebrew words to get a good understanding of the meaning. (I.e. look up "eyes were weak", "form", "face")

14. According to Ruth 4:11, for what are Rachel and Leah remembered?

15. NAMES Research:

Rachel –

Leah –

Reuben –

Simeon –

Levi –

Judah –

Gad –

Asher –

Issachar –

Zebulun –

Dinah –

Israel –

Dan –

Naphtali –

Joseph –

Ben-oni –

Benjamin –

JOCHEBED and MIRIAM

Scripture References – Ex. 2:1-10; Ex. 6:20; Num. 26:59; Ex. 15:20-21; Num. 12; Hebrews 11:23

16. NAMES Research.

Amram –

Jochebed –

Miriam –

Aaron –

Moses –

17. The Pharaoh said to _____ all baby boys born to the _____. (Ex.1:22)

18. What did this woman do with her son? (Ex.2:1-3)

19. Read Romans 13:1-2. Should we obey the government? YES or NO

     If "yes", was Jochebed (Num. 26:59) right to hide her son? (Acts 5:29)

20. What did Miriam do to help her mother and brother? (Ex. 2:4)

21. In whom did Jochebed put her trust? (Hebrews 11:23)

22. What role was Miriam sent to fulfill? (Ex.15:20, 21; Micah 6:4)

23. In Numbers 12:1-15 Aaron and Miriam are upset with Moses and speak disrespectfully to and about him.

What was the reason for their disapproval?

What did they say was bothering them?

How was Miriam punished?

Conclusion: Take a quick glance at these women:

Rebekah's story started with her being a benefit to her husband and ended with her deceiving him to elevate her favorite son.

Rachel was physically beautiful and had Jacob's love – yet she was not content with what she had. Her jealousy marred her relationship with her sister and her husband.

Leah was blessed with many children, but her discontent led her to join in the fight with Rachel over Jacob. She was no longer loving, but desiring to possess.

We only know of one story about Jochebed, but look what her faith and ingenuity gave us!

Miriam was a helper, protector, prophetess, and yet lost the promised land.

So, what do we take from these women? Find the GOOD in each one, and imitate it. Notice the WRONG in each one, and avoid it! Go back to James 4:7 'Therefore submit to God. Resist the devil and he will flee from you." Life is about making choices – choose to dwell on the good things and glorify God. 1 Timothy 4:16 says, "Take heed to yourself and to the doctrine. Continue in them, for in doing this you will save both yourself and those who hear you." Your beauty, your past good behavior, your abundance compared to others' lack is something in which you should never put your faith and trust. Be like Jochebed and trust that the Lord will protect you when you do what pleases Him.

In Your Bible:

Genesis 46; 48:7; 49:31

Numbers 20:1

Deuteronomy 24:9

1 Chronicles 6:3

Jeremiah 31:15

Micah 6:4

Matthew 2:18

2 Timothy 3:14-15

Study Builders

Use this page to note all the verses from the lesson into one or more of the categories.

In Manner of Life In Purity	In Word
In Love	In Faith

Additional Notes:

Lesson 6

True Beauty

"Beauty is only skin deep."

"Pretty is as pretty does."

There are many things that the world says about beauty. Magazines, books, music and movies attempt to define it. Fashion attempts to improve upon it. Makeup tries to enhance it. Salons try to sell it. Our world is obsessed with "beautiful" as though it is something you can purchase and be proud of owning it. As is often the case, the world has things backward. Let's take a look at how God defines beauty, because His word is TRUTH (Ps.119:160; Jn. 17:17). We can TRUST that His definition will be of benefit to each one of us (Deut. 6:24).

Don't forget to be filling out your STUDY BUILDERS as we go along!

Start with a basic definition of BEAUTY.

Beauty [byoo-tee]

1. The quality present in a thing or person that gives intense pleasure or deep satisfaction to the mind, whether arising from sensory manifestations (as shape, color, sound, etc.), a meaningful design or pattern, or something else (as a personality in which high spiritual qualities are manifest).   (from www.dictionary.com)

Let's begin with some things that are not beautiful.

Read Matthew 23:27-28.

1. What was wrong with the Scribes and Pharisees?

2. How does Jesus describe them?

3. Write Luke 6:43-45 here.

Read Mark 7:14-23.

4. What proceeds out of the heart of men? (12 things)

5. Let's make sure that we know what some of those words mean:

Define:

Covetousness –

Sensuality (lewdness) –

Envy (evil eye) –

Pride –

Foolishness –

Let's think about our physical beauty and the things we do to have it. Do you think it's possible for you to be guilty of the above sins in regards to your beauty? Can you be greedy about the clothes you wear?   What about in how many outfits you have; wanting an outfit that another woman has, but not wanting to be seen as wearing the same things? Can you be envious of others? Can you be guilty of wanting to MAKE others envious? Think about specific situations that would fall into those listed sins. This way you can be prepared to AVOID these things.

6. Explain what Proverbs 11:22 means.

Here is an example of physical beauty used for evil purposes.

Read 2 Kings 9.

7. What mission did God give to Jehu? (verse 7-10)

Jehu is on a rampage – he is striking people down right and left.

8. In verse 30, how does Jezebel respond to the threat of the coming new king of Israel?

(We will talk about her more later on, but for now, look up what the name Jezebel means – interesting don't you think?)

Read Ezekiel 16:11-16

9. Who had made Jerusalem beautiful and a place famous among the nations?

10. How did Jerusalem respond with the gifts God had given her? (verse15-16)

11. In Ezekiel 23:40-41 how had these people used wealthy clothes and makeup?

We can see that things like clothes, jewelry, and makeup were further indicators of God's blessings on His people. The people unfortunately then began to think that their "beauty" was of their own doing! We must be wary of following in their footsteps (Hebrews 4:11).

12. In Jeremiah 4:30, Jeremiah describes how the nation will try to cover up its destruction. What illustration does he use to make the point?

••

Now let's look at what God sees as beautiful!

Read Genesis 1:31.

13. God made Eve (and everything else) and it was _____. (two words)

14. In Genesis 2:21-25 we are told of how God created Eve. From these verses, what are we told about her physical appearance? Is that significant?

Read Jeremiah 18:4-11; Isaiah 61:10

15. Who makes you beautiful (a good thing) – you or God?

16. In Proverbs 20:15, what is a precious jewel?

17. In Romans 10:15, who are said to have "beautiful" feet and what does that mean?

18. How did holy women adorn themselves in former times, according to 1 Peter 3:4-5?

19. What is "precious" in the sight of God? (1 Peter 3:4)

Read 1 Timothy 2:8-11.

20. Paul teaches Timothy how to teach women to "adorn themselves". How is the apparel described?

21. In verse 11, it says, this is proper (apparel) for who?

These verses CONNECT what you WEAR with HOW you BEHAVE or WHAT you DO. Let's look at how people were IDENTIFIED by the CLOTHING they wore.

Read Genesis 38:14, 15

22. Notice two things here –

     a. Tamar took off her what? (verse 14)

     b. Tamar put on what and this made her look like what? (verse 15)

Read 2 Samuel 13:18.

23. What did Tamar wear that identified her separate from other women?

It is not wrong that people associate a look with a behavior – it's just a fact that they will. You must do what you can to NOT be mistaken for the wrong thing. You are in control of how people see you, most of the time. "First impressions are everything." There's a reason that people say that. What someone SEES when they first meet you is a huge part of what they will THINK about you when they walk away. What IMPRESSION do you want to leave?

As a reminder from our lesson about AUTHORITY –

24. According to Isaiah 29:16, who tells whom what to do?

25. According to 1 Corinthians 6:19, 20, if you are a Christian, who does your body belong to?

Doesn't that contradict the cry of the world that abortion is not murder because a woman can do with her body whatever she wants?

26. Does Romans 6:12, 13 say that it's ok to sin occasionally, because we "just can't help it, it's natural"?

Read Matthew 6:25-34.

27. After reading these verses, how much concern do you think God wants you to have about your hair, your face, or your clothes?

The verses are talking about God providing for your NEEDS. Do we sometimes put "wants" into the "needs" category? What should we do instead?

There are so many verses we could look at that describe just how God wants us to be. In the following list, write next to each verse what it is that would make us "beautiful" as God would have us to be.

A. John 15:4

B. Romans 8:9-11

C. Ephesians 5:15

D. Philippians 2:5

E. Colossians 1:10

F. 2 Thessalonians 1:11-12

G. Hebrews 13:20-21

H. 2 John 6

I. 3 John 3

J. 2 Peter 3:18

Conclusion:

God's definition of beauty is FAR DEEPER than ANYTHING the world tries to sell to us. There may be appreciation for the way something looks, but this isn't the beauty that God wants you to be SEEKING. He's given us the added benefits of plants that can be made into wonderful fabrics or dyes. He's shown man the beauty of refined gold and silver. But He NEVER gave us those things to bring GLORY to OURSELVES. They are to bring glory to HIM. When we forget THAT – we've lost that TRUE BEAUTY that we were SEEKING already.

So, what do you think? Does it matter why you wear makeup, or how much? Is it important that you choose clothing that goes further than what the world thinks is modest? How much of YOU are you trying to show and how much of HIM?

Study Builders

Use this page to note all the verses from the lesson into one or more of the categories.

In Manner of Life In Purity	In Word
In Love	In Faith

Additional Notes:

Lesson 7

Lessons from a Harlot, a Prophet Judge, and Young Widow

(Rahab, Deborah, and Ruth)

Scripture References: Joshua 2, 6; Matt.1:5 Heb. 11:31; James 2:25; Judges 4, 5; Book of Ruth

Did you know that the world teaches that God, in the Bible, has a degrading view of women? You don't have to look very far to see that many believe that God's story in the Bible puts women into a subservient position, that it glorifies MAN over WOMAN, and that God wants women to be nothing more than baby machines. If you haven't noticed it so far in this study, I do believe this is one lesson that can prove that point absolutely FALSE! God holds women up – not higher than men, but equal with them. All men AND women in scripture are shown to have faults (excepting Jesus, of course) and strengths – some more than others. "Then Peter opened his mouth and said; 'In truth I perceive that God shows no partiality'" (Acts 10:34 NKJV). You are your own person with your own mind – do not take my word for it. Read GOD'S WORD and understand what the TRUTH is.

Rahab

Joshua 2, 6; Matthew 1:5; Hebrews 11:31; and James 2:25

1. What did Rahab do for the spies?

2. What did she know (Joshua 2:11)?

3. There was an agreement made that would bring about Rahab's salvation. What was her part? (Joshua 2:17-20)

4. Why did Rahab "not perish along with those who were disobedient"? (Hebrews 11:31)

Read Joshua 2:21; 6:17, 22-25.

5. In Joshua 6:23, we read Rahab, her father, her mother, and her brothers and all she had was saved. This happened because both parties to the agreement kept their part completely.   TRUE or FALSE

6. Would Rahab's belief that God "is God in heaven above and on earth beneath" have done her any good if she had not followed the spies instructions? (James 2:25-26; Hebrews 11:6)

Deborah

Scripture References: Judges 4 and 5

7. Why did Israel need a judge? (Judges 4:1-3)

8. List the titles we know Deborah wore (Judges 4:4; 5:7)

    1.

    2.

    3.

    4.

9. Deborah intended to go out to war herself, just like the male judges before her. (Judges 4:5-7)   TRUE or FALSE

10. What prophecy does Deborah make in Judges 4:9?

11. Was Jael's house on Israel's side or the King of Canaan's? (Judges 4:11, 12, 17)

12. How is Jael remembered for what she did? (Judges 5:24-27)

Read Judges 5.

13. Verse 31 says, "let those who love Him be like the rising of the sun in its might". Who showed their love for the Lord and their brethren?

14. Who did not?

15. Deborah and Barak accepted all the credit for defeating Jabin the King of Canaan.

TRUE or FALSE

Ruth

Scripture References the Book of Ruth

16. Why did Elimilech go to Moab?

17. In a short paragraph, tell the story of Naomi and her family while in Moab.

18. After Naomi decides to return to Bethlehem, what do Orpah and Ruth do?

19. NAMES Research:

Elimelech –

Naomi –

Mahlon –

Chilion –

Orpah –

Ruth –

Boaz –

Obed –

20. What attitude does Ruth show now that she lives in Bethlehem? (Ruth 2:2)

21. Who notices Ruth?

22. What had Boaz heard about Ruth? (Ruth 2:11-12)

Ruth had a REPUTATION! Did it make a difference what that reputation reflected about her? Absolutely!

23. Naomi tells Ruth to put on expensive clothes and makeup to go before Boaz. (Ruth 3:3)   TRUE or FALSE

24. Who is Boaz's mother? (Matt.1:5)

25. Now that Ruth has married Boaz, Naomi must find somewhere else to live in her old age.   TRUE or FALSE

26. Fill in the blanks.

   Ruth was _____ than _____ sons. (Ruth 4:15)

27. Who is Ruth's great-grandson? (Ruth 4:17)

Conclusion:

WHAT GLORIOUS WOMEN!

These three women teach us about how obedience is very important to God. Rahab and her family would have been destroyed in Jericho without it. Those who fought to save Israel under Deborah and Barak were commended for it. Ruth would not have been protected if she hadn't followed Naomi in obeying the laws of Moses.

These women all recognized God's AUTHORITY and submitted to it. They weren't made less because of this – they were HONORED and HERALDED through the ages!

Recognize your need like Rahab; be confident in your abilities like Deborah; seize the opportunity like Jael; see God's hand in your life like Naomi; and live like you appreciate your blessings as Ruth did!

Study Builders

Use this page to note all the verses from the lesson into one or more of the categories.

In Manner of Life In Purity	In Word
In Love	In Faith

Additional Notes:

<u>Lesson 8</u>

<u>Four Queens</u>

<u>(Vashti, Esther, Jezebel, and Athaliah)</u>

Scripture References: Book of Esther; 1 Kings 16:31; 1 Kings 18, 19, 21; 1 Kings 22:52; 2 Kings 9; Rev. 2:20; 2 Kings 8:18. 26-27; 2 Kings 11; 2 Chron. 22, 23

<u>Vashti</u>

1. Why did King Ahasuerus give a banquet in the third year of his reign? (Esther 1:3-4)

2. In what condition was the King on the 7th day of his final banquet? (Esther 1:10)

3. What did he ask the eunuchs to do? (Esther 1:10-11)

4. How did Vashti respond? (Esther 1:12)

There are many views about Vashti's response. One is that the King was asking her to appear ONLY with her crown on, and that this would be degrading and immoral to her. Another is that Persian traditions held that the head Queen would be MORE secluded than any other woman in the court, because of her value and stature. To parade her before others might have been so unheard of and unexpected that she wouldn't have complied. You can search the internet, bible dictionaries, or almanacs for "Vashti in the book of Esther" and see what they say. But always remember – what MATTERS is what the BIBLE says. If it's not explained, we don't need to know, period (Deut. 29:29).

5. How did the King feel about her refusal? (Esther 1:12)

6. The King's advisors told him what the law was about disobeying the command of the King. (Esther 1:15-20)   TRUE or FALSE

7. Instead of following the current law, what did Ahasuerus do? (Esther 1:19-22)

<u>Esther</u>

8. Tell the story of how Esther (Hadassah) comes to be Queen.

9. Some Math!

In what year of the King's reign did Esther become Queen (Esther 2:16)?

In what year did Vashti fall out of favor (Esther 1:3)?

How many years had the King been without a Queen?

10. In Esther 2:17, what did the King feel/show towards Esther more than towards the other girls?

11. How did others respond to Esther? (Esther 2:8-9, 15)

12. What was Esther's attitude toward Mordecai? (Esther 2:10, 20)

13. What was Mordecai's belief about why Esther was chosen as Queen? (Esther 4:14)

14. What is Esther's first action in dealing with the problem that is brought before her? (Esther 4:16)

(For more about Fasting and prayer going together, see Ezra 8:23; Psalm 35:13; Daniel 9:3; Matthew 17:21; Mark 9:29; 1 Corinthians 7:5)

15. What was Esther's attitude toward the King? (Esther 4:11; 5:1, 4, 8; 7:3, 4; 8:3-6)

Notice how Esther does not change when she's granted power. She remembers her "place", aka she remembers the KING'S rightful place, always.

Jezebel

Read Revelation 2:20.

16. If this was the first time you'd heard the name Jezebel, what would you think about it?

Now let's see what the "original" Jezebel was all about.

17. In 1 Kings 16:31, how does scripture describe Jezebel?

18. How did Obadiah feel about Jezebel? (1 Kings 18:3-4)

19. Who did Jezebel associate with? (1 Kings 18:19)

20. How did Jezebel respond to her prophets being killed? (1 Kings 19:1-3)

21. How did Elijah feel about Jezebel? (1 Kings 19:3, 4)

22. Read 1 Kings 21:5-10. Does Jezebel advise Ahab or take over the problem herself?

23. Is her answer to the problem a just (righteous) one? (see 1 Kings 21:14-16)

24. Is only Jezebel held accountable for what happens to Naboth?

What does this teach you about how God sees things? What about when a friend does something to someone else on your behalf that is not nice? Is the idea of "my hands aren't dirty so I'm not to blame" a valid one? (See also Matthew 27:19-26)

25. Read 2 Kings 9:30-37. What stands out to you about Jezebel's behavior?

What is she responding to in this moment?

Athaliah

26. What influence did Athaliah have on Joram, King of Judah? (2 Kings 8:17-18)

27. What is the legacy of the "house of Ahab"? (2 Kings 8:26-27)

28. How did the people feel about Athaliah after her 6-year reign of terror? (2 Kings 11:20)

Notice how little information there is about Jezebel and Athaliah – but really what else do we NEED to know? Read Mark 7:20-23 and see how Jezebel and Athaliah match up to this list! This is where you should see a huge "DANGER THIS WAY" sign! God is about balance – He shows us the right way to be AND He shows us how NOT to be! "Take note, and see what you should do," (1 Kings 20:22).

Conclusion:

What LEGACY will be remembered because of you and your actions? Doing the right thing at the right time like Esther? Being so vile that other evil people are compared to you, like Jezebel? Or being cut throat enough to kill your own grandchildren like Athaliah?

These women show, above all, how others responded to their behavior. How do others respond to you? What do they think of you? What type of behavior do you encourage in others by your example?

If you're unhappy with what they see – what are you going to change to make it better?

There is a difference in not being liked for doing what is right, like Jesus (Is. 53:3) and just not being liked or likeable. Pay attention and make the most of the opportunities that you have so you may be improved by the refining that comes from God's word (Ps. 66:10).

Study Builders

Use this page to note all the verses from the lesson into one or more of the categories.

In Manner of Life In Purity	In Word
In Love	In Faith

Additional Notes:

Lesson 9

The Company that You Keep

What is one point that continues to come up in each lesson? That life is all about your CHOICES! The people you choose to be around is very important no matter what stage of life you are in.

Read Psalm 1:1-4

1. List the negative associations mentioned here.

    a.

    b.

    c.

2. List the positives of staying away from these people given in the verses.

    a.

    b.

    c.

    d.

3. Read James 1:23-24. Tell me in your own words what these verses are telling us.

There's a commercial about people who have an illness but they ignore it, hoping it will go away. In the commercial these people are in line at the bank, or the store, and they have a huge snake wrapped around their leg or arm. People around them ask them about it, they say they are just ignoring it or will deal with it later. What do you think the point of the commercial is?

Does forgetting we have a problem make it go away or make it better?

We have to look at these things with a desire and intent (there are those CHOICES again) to correct ourselves so that we'll be right with God.

4. Read 2 Timothy 2:22. What does God tell us to flee?

5. What does He tell us to pursue?

6. With whom should we pursue them?

See what I mean about God and balance? In ONE verse, He tells us what to avoid, what to seek after, and WHO to spend our time with doing the seeking! Simple!

7. According to Matthew 6:24, which two things can we serve?

8. Can we serve them at the same time?

9. Read 2 Corinthians 6:14-18. What does "unequally yoked" give us a picture of?

10. "Unbelievers" are equated with six things. List them here.

      a.

      b.

      c.

      d.

      e.

      f.

11. Read Proverbs 4:20-27. What is the final choice mentioned in verse 27?

12. Read Proverbs 7:6-7, 24-27. We can always trust that we will be strong enough to avoid falling into sin.   TRUE or FALSE

13. Proverbs 1:10-19. This is a vivid description to make a strong point. What is the sin being specifically described? (verse 19)

14. Describe one way you could "deceive" yourself in regards to the friends that you choose (1 Corinthians 15:33-34).

15. Galatians 6:1-2. This verse is easy to fulfill, no matter who my friends might be.

TRUE or FALSE

16. What was the reason given for Israel to not marry into the nations around them (Deuteronomy 7:3-4)?

Read 2 Corinthians 10:12, 13

17. What was wrong with those who "commend themselves"?

18. Paul says not to "boast beyond measure". How do we know where the limits are?

19. To whom or what should we compare ourselves?

20. Read 1 Corinthians 5:11 and 2 Thessalonians 3:14. Can you have an influence on your friends by how you react to their choices?

21. Read Romans 16:17-19. Can people who do not serve Christ have an influence on their friends who do?

22. Read Ephesians 6:10-17

Describe the armor talked about in these verses.

What is the armor to help us do?

Why do you think God described salvation as a helmet?

Why do you think God described faith as a shield?

Why do you think God said the word of God is a sword?

The Lord has provided a way for you to PROTECT yourself and to FIGHT against those evil influences Satan will send your way.

Read 1 Peter 5:8-9.

23. The devil really isn't very interested in you.   TRUE or FALSE

24. Are you alone in having to face these battles?

25. Write a prayer asking for God to help you make good choices about the people around you, the places you go, and the things that you do.

Conclusion:

We are in a BATTLE against the vices of Satan and we need help to be STRONG: help from God, help from the Word, and help from others who are going the same way we are going (Matthew 7:13-14).

Choose carefully who you will serve (Joshua 24:15) AND those with whom you will serve!

In Your Bible:
1 Thess. 5:21-22
James 1:2, 3
1 Thess. 5:11
Gal. 6:9
Exodus 23:2

Study Builders

Use this page to note all the verses from the lesson into one or more of the categories.

In Manner of Life In Purity	In Word
In Love	In Faith

Additional Notes:

Lesson 10

Be Strong and of Good Courage

Do you ever have a day where you just want to pull the covers back over your head and hide? Have you ever avoided doing something new, just because you were afraid of how it would turn out?   Everyone has had these feelings at one time or another. YOU ARE NOT ALONE! But we feel as though we are sometimes. We hesitate because we lack CONFIDANCE and our COURAGE wans. At this point in our study, it's good to remind ourselves of how to find that strength and courage that will get us up out of bed, help us to face our fears, and to walk upright – no matter what the rest of the world may be doing. The promises of 2 Timothy 3:17 and 2 Peter 1:3 cover these concerns too, you know!

1. Write Psalm 121:7, 8 here.

Read Psalm 91

2. What does verse one give you a mental picture of?

3. Does verse two make you believe that God is strong or only strong sometimes?

4. What does verse four make you think of?

5. What does verse nine say the Lord has for you?

6. What protection is promised in verse eleven?

7. In verses 14-16, why does God say He protects this way?

8. 2 Peter 1:4-11: List the things that Peter says to do so that "you will never stumble".

9. God makes it hard for us to know what He wants us to do.   TRUE or FALSE

Read Psalm 34:4

10. Does David believe God heard him when he prayed?

11. What did the Lord do for David?

Read Isaiah 41:10.

12. What does the Lord promise here?

13. How does that knowledge make you feel?

14. Can you name some characters in the Bible who God helped through scary situations?

Read Psalm 118:6.

15. Who is on your side?

16. Look at Romans 8:31 – does this sound the same as the verse in Psalms?

Read Isaiah 41:13.

17. What does the Lord say?

Read Psalm 121:7, 8.
18. Do you think the Lord is only watching you once in a while?

There are people in the world who believe that God is "busy" and that sometimes He just can't hear us or be bothered by us. Also there are some who believe that God stepped back from us after Creation and that He really has no interest in us beyond that.

19. After what you've been reading, do you believe that to be true?

Read Isaiah 5:20.
20. Can you think of some examples of people doing what is talked about in this verse?

Read Psalm 31:24.
21. Who is promised the help in this verse?

22. Read Deuteronomy Chapter 31. How many times does Moses say "be strong and of good courage" or something similar?

23. Read Joshua Chapter 1. How many times does Joshua say "be strong and of good courage" or something similar?

24. In 1 Chronicles 28:20, who did David say would be with Solomon as he finished the work of the Temple?

25. According to 2 Peter 3:17-18, what can you do to "be on your guard" (NASB) or "beware"?

26. Write 1 Corinthians 16:13 here.

27. Write a prayer thanking God for His care for you and asking for the courage to stand when it is scary to do so.

Conclusion:

Courage or bravery is a choice. It's not something that you either are or are not. Being brave is something you DO. Courage and bravery are NOT being unafraid of things. Courage is standing up when you are afraid. Fear is not a bad thing; letting fear control you so that you don't do the right thing is bad. Think of the people in scripture who showed courage: Jesus – He was afraid in the garden before His crucifixion, but He went on and let them take Him away, hurt Him, and then kill Him. He could have called for help to stop it all – but He didn't. David stood in the face of lions, bears, and King Saul – not without fear, but with courage and the Lord on his side. What about Esther? Did it take courage to do what she did? Can you think of any others?

We should be able to do as Hebrews 13:6 says,
     "So we may BOLDLY say: 'The Lord is MY helper; I will not fear. What can man do to me?'" (emphasis mine, ADL)

In Your Bible:

Psalm 91:11   2 Samuel 10:12 and 2 Chronicles 19:13

Hebrews 1:13, 14   Ephesians 6:10

Isaiah 40:29   1 Chronicles 22:13

Psalm 23:4   2 Timothy 2:1

Joshua 10:25   John 14:27

Psalm 27:14   Proverbs 3:5-6

Study Builders

Use this page to note all the verses from the lesson into one or more of the categories.

In Manner of Life In Purity	In Word
In Love	In Faith

Additional Notes:

Lesson 11

Prayer and a Thankful Attitude

"Rejoice always, pray without ceasing, in everything give thanks; for this is the will of God in Christ Jesus for you." 1 Thessalonians 5:16-18

Lesson over! Ok, maybe not. Notice again how God gives us everything we need! Isn't that fascinating to you? I love it, obviously. God doesn't leave it there, although He could. As we've seen before, repetition of ideas creates EMPHASIS. Let's explore more of what He's seen fit to teach us on this matter.

Read Psalm 100.

1. Why should we be thankful to the Lord?

2. When you read these verses what emotion do they show?

3. According to Psalm 30:12, how long did David say he would thank God?

Read 1 Thessalonians 5:18

4. Is saying "thank you" something we do only because we want to?

5. Is it sinful to not be thankful?

Read Ephesians 5:20

6. We give thanks to God in the "name of" who?

7. Do you know what that means?

We are ABLE to give thanks to God BECAUSE of the ACCESS we have to Him THROUGH Jesus Christ (1 Peter 2:5; Ephesians 3:12). If we are not IN Jesus Christ (Galatians 3:27) we do not have this access (John 14:6). It is a precious thing, something in and of itself for which we should be thankful!

8. What is mercy?

9. How long does God's mercy last? (1 Chronicles 16:34)

I want to consider a few specific things regarding prayer. Again – God has given us EVERYTHING WE NEED, we just have to LOOK for it and ACCEPT it as TRUTH.
You may be thinking, "But I don't really know HOW to pray."

Hmm, let's see if the scriptures cover that one. (Some of the following information I found compiled in a book called "Girls, Girls, Girls" by Mrs. A.R. Hill, Sr.)

Luke 11:1 "Lord teach us to pray…" – see someone else needed to know how when Jesus was here teaching.

Use the verses to answer the following:

10. When, or how often, should I pray?
    A. 1 Thess. 5:17
    B. Acts 2:42
    C. James 5:13-15
    D. Mark 1:35
    E. Luke 6:12
    F. Daniel 6:10

11. Where should I, can I, pray?
    A. 1 Timothy 2:8
    B. Luke 5:16
    C. Matthew 14:23
    D. Luke 18:10
    E. Acts 12:12
    F. Luke 3:21
    G. Matthew 26:36 (with John 18:1-3)
    H. Matthew 6:6

12. Who can pray?
    A. James 5:16; Psalm 34:17
    B. James 1:5
    C. Matthew 7:11

13. Did we miss anything? Look up "pray", "prayer", "praying", and "prayed" in your concordance and see what other answers you can find for each one. (A hint for if you're using an electronic concordance, internet site, or application – if you type in pray* - it will give you all the verses that include any form of the word "pray".)

Another question you may ask, are there good prayers and bad prayers, and does it matter?

Again, use the verses to find the answers.

14. Conditions of Acceptable Prayer.
    1. James 1:6; Hebrews 11:6; Mark 11:24
    2. John 14:14; James 5:14
    3. 1 John 5:14
    4. Matthew 6:12-14

15. Wasted Prayers (prayers that won't be heard)
1. Psalm 66:18
2. Proverbs 28:9
3. Matthew 6:5
4. Matthew 6:7
5.   James 4:3
6.   Luke 18:9-14
7.   James 1:6-7

16. Do a search in your concordance for variations of "thank" (thank, thanks, thankful, etc.). You could look for "gratitude" and "grateful" too. How many times does this concept occur in scripture?

17. Choose three verses, (preferably not already in the lesson), for pray* and thank* to add to your Study Builders.

Conclusion:

Praying is not just talking – it's talking to someone important, who deserves that you consider what you say before you speak. There are many other aspects to PRAYER that we haven't touched on here. You can explore that on your own by doing a word study of the synonyms for prayer throughout scripture.

"Be anxious for nothing, but in everything by prayer and supplication, with thanksgiving, let your requests be made known to God; and the peace of God, which surpasses all understanding, will guard your hearts and minds through Christ Jesus." Philippians 4:6-7

What an AMAZING PROMISE! We've talked before about WHO God is, WHO Jesus is, and the AUTHORITY that GOD has because we are His CREATION. We should say prayers of PRAISE; telling Him how wonderful we KNOW Him to be. We should say prayers of SUPPLICATION to ask for the needs of OTHERS and ourselves. ALL of our prayers should be with THANKSGIVING, ALWAYS.

And as for application, your THANKFULNESS should carry over into all aspects of your life. You should never feel so entitled that you would DARE to walk around feeling unhappy and ungrateful for the life that has been given to you – by the Lord and the hard work and loving care of others. If thankfulness is hard for you and complaining is easy (if you're uncertain as to which is true about you – ask your mother. ☺) – make a list. Write down on one side of a piece of paper all the things you think are not worthy of your happiness. On the other side of that piece of paper, write down all of the things, start with what's within your immediate area, which you have or have access to through NO EFFORT OF YOUR OWN.

Just in case you need an example to help you out –

<u>I don't like…</u>	<u>Blessings</u>

the comforter on my bed, (the colors aren't "cool" anymore) so I need a new one	the bed in my room
	   mattress
	  bed covering to keep me warm
	  pajamas/clothes to sleep in
	  electricity for light in my room
	    light bulb in the fixture
	    pillow
	    sheets

Do you see where I'm going? For the majority of us, we have far MORE than we NEED. To wake up and feel as though you are owed more just simply does NOT go along with any scripture we've studied thus far. So get up, SMILE, COUNT YOUR BLESSINGS, and be THANKFUL to those in your life and to the LORD who gave it to you in the first place!

Study Builders

Use this page to note all the verses from the lesson into one or more of the categories.

In Manner of Life In Purity	In Word
In Love	In Faith

Additional Notes:

Lesson 12

Forgiveness

"Forgive and forget."

Easier said than done sometimes, isn't it? Forgiveness is an important thing to consider though. Especially when put in the context of just how much each and every one of us is forgiven by God when we accept His gift of grace (Titus 2:11-14; Ephesians 1:7). Forgiveness is a gift you can give to others, but it is also a gift to yourself. Forgiveness is FREEDOM, and we've been "called to freedom" (Galatians 5:13). Let's study to find a way to make that phrase, "Forgive and forget", easier done.

1. According to Matthew 7:12, how are we to treat others?

Peter asked about forgiveness in Matthew 18:21-22 and Luke 17:3, 4.

2. How many times was forgiveness asked for?

3. How many times was it to be given?

4. What three things go together in Luke 17:3-4?

Jesus uses a parable to make His point about forgiveness very clear in Matthew 18:23-35.

5. What had the Master done? (verses 25-27)

6. This story uses some exaggeration to make the point. Explain the extreme circumstances that are compared. (verses 24 and 28)

7. Define "compassion".

8. What do we lose if we won't forgive others? (Matthew 6:14-15)

9. Fill in the blank.

"And be _____ to one another, _____, _____ one another, even as God _____ _____ forgave you."   Ephesians 4:32

10. Write Colossians 3:13 here.

Let's consider that one for a minute. "Even as God in Christ forgave you" and "as Christ forgave you"; what exactly does that mean?

10. Who is God "ready to forgive" in Psalm 86:5?

11. What did God expect from Israel before He would "forgive their sin and heal their land"? (2 Chronicles 7:14)

12. How does God forgive (justify, give life)? Use the verses to find the answers.

      a. Romans 3:23-24

      b. Romans 8:32

      c. 1 Corinthians 2:12

      d. Revelation 21:6

      e. Revelation 22:17

13. Does God expect something from us before He "freely" gives His forgiveness? (1 John 1:9; Acts 2:38)

So we are to forgive others in the same way that God forgives us – freely. God doesn't forgive us without our repentance, but He is patiently waiting for us to repent so He can forgive us (Acts 17:30-31; Acts 26:17-18). God wipes the slate clean for us when we repent (Col.2:13). We have no other way to "undo" all the things we do against Him. It isn't something He wastes on those who have no use for it (Luke 15:11-32).

Conclusion:

Is it right for you to expect your parents and friends to forgive you if you have never said, "I'm sorry I..."? On the flip side, do you want to be treated harshly until you say those words in just the right way? If you've done wrong to someone – humble yourself and admit your wrong and ask for forgiveness (James 5:16). If someone does wrong toward you, pray for them (Luke 6:28), and be ready with forgiveness when they come to you. You may even need to make the first step, by bringing it up to them (Matthew 18:15). Your own lack of forgiveness can get in the way of your worship being received by God (Matthew 5:23, 24), and as we've already mentioned can keep you from being forgiven by God! It's a blight that you want to remove from your own life, and should want to help remove from someone else's life when it's in your power to do so. You can't forgive their sins as God can, but you can forgive their mistakes towards you – just a further reach of the blessing of forgiveness that began before Creation and was sealed on the Cross!

Study Builders

Use this page to note all the verses from the lesson into one or more of the categories.

In Manner of Life In Purity	In Word
In Love	In Faith

Additional Notes:

Lesson 13

Speech Problems

"Sticks and stones may break my bones, but words can never hurt me."

Have you ever said that? Why did you say it? Probably to someone who has said something not so nice to you to let them know you're not fazed by what they said. The truth is words do hurt, but they also can do good.

"Who sharpen their tongue like a sword, and bend their bows to shoot their arrows – bitter words." Psalm 64:3

"Pleasant words are like a honeycomb, Sweetness to the soul and health to the bones." Proverb 16:24

This is another choice for you – how you USE your words. Let's go looking for what God has to say about SPEECH PROBLEMS.

Read James 3:5-18.

1. James taught that what we say doesn't harm anything or anyone.   TRUE or FALSE

2. Read Matthew 15:11-18. (We've read this before.) How does this scripture go along with the one in James?

3. According to John 8:44, who is the father of lying?

4. Read Genesis 3:1-4. How many words did it take to make Satan's statement a lie?

5. Tell how lying played a part in the story of Jacob and Esau from when we studied Rebekah.

6. Cain's murder of Abel left him open to do what in Genesis 4:9?

Read Acts 5:1-11.

7. What lie did Ananias and Sapphira tell?

8. Were they trying to do a good thing?

9. Did that make lying about it all right?

10. Read Proverb 6:16-19. Seven things the Lord hates – how many are done by the tongue (speech)?

11. In Proverbs 10:18-21 there is a series of things about words. Use the verses to answer the following:

Hiding hatred is _____.

Spreading slander is _____. (Slander is a spoken false statement that

damages the reputation.)

Talking a lot makes opportunity for _____.

Being quiet is _____.

The value of words from the righteous person is as _____.

The value of the heart (thoughts) of the wicked person is _____.

Righteous words are a benefit to _____ while fools die for lack of

_____.

I think we understand that lying is not good. Let's see about GOSSIP.

12. Write Proverb 11:13 here.

13. What is "gossip" or "tale bearing"?

14. Is it normal that people like to hear the things that are said in gossip? (Prov. 18:8)

15. Does our liking to listen to it make it RIGHT to listen?

16. What does stopping gossip do? (Prov. 26:20)

17. Proverb 20:19 repeats the idea that "a talebearer reveals secrets" and adds a command. How would flattery and gossip go together?

18. According to 1Timothy 5:13, 14, how can a young widow avoid being a gossip and busybody? (This doesn't only apply to young widows. ☺)

19. Gossip is not a very serious sin compared to something like murder. (Rom.1:28-32)   TRUE or FALSE

20. What is "flattery"?

21. What company does flattering speech keep in Psalm 5:8, 9?

22. Read Psalm 12:1-4; Prov. 26:28; and 1 Thess. 2:5. Flattery is a valid way to build someone up.   TRUE or FALSE

We've covered talking about OTHER people, what about talking about OURSELVES?

23. Read Proverb 25:14. Explain this proverb in your own words.

24. It is always best that you let others know about your own accomplishments. (Prov.27:2)   TRUE or FALSE

Are you noticing that WORDS can do harm? I often tell my daughters to "use their words". Words are POWERFUL. We MUST be careful with them. Words reveal the hidden person of the heart – whether righteous or not. CHOOSE your words carefully. Speak to others the way you'd like to be spoken to.

"For all the law is fulfilled in one word, even in this: 'You shall love your neighbor as yourself.' But if you bite and devour one another, beware lest you be consumed by one another."   Galatians 5:14-15

Some BENEFITS of SOUND words.

Declares righteousness, promotes health, is established forever – Proverbs 12:17-19

Turns away wrath – Proverb 15:1

Is a tree of LIFE – Proverb 15:4

Conclusion:

The cure for an out of control tongue:

Confession and prayer – James 5:16

THINK BEFORE YOU SPEAK!

Treat others the way you want to be treated – Matthew 7:12

Fill your mind with GOOD THINGS – Philippians 4:8

Use your words to BENEFIT OTHERS rather than yourself – Rom. 14:19; 1 Thess. 5:11

In Your Bible –

Proverb 8:13	Proverb 10:32	Proverb 29:5
Proverb 12:22	Proverb 13:3, 5	Proverb 21:9, 19
Proverb 28:23	Proverb 26:22	Proverb 16:28
Proverb 25:15		

Study Builders

Use this page to note all the verses from the lesson into one or more of the categories.

In Manner of Life In Purity	In Word
In Love	In Faith

Additional Notes:

Lesson 14

Lessons from Hannah and Three Wives of King David (Michal, Bathsheba, Abigail)

<u>Hannah</u>

Scripture Reference: 1Samuel 1-2:20

1. Who was Hannah?

2. What did she want?

3. What did she do about her problem?

4. Hannah only talked to God about her problem every now and then?
   TRUE or FALSE

5. What was Hannah doing that made Eli, the priest, think she was drunk?

6. What was Hannah's response to Eli's prophecy?

7. What was Hannah's response after the prophecy was fulfilled?

8. Did Hannah regret the vow she had made to God? (1 Samuel 1:27-28)

We see here, again, LEGACY. Legacy is not only physical things; it's our actions, our words, our lives. Build yours carefully.

<u>Michal</u>

Scripture References: 1 Samuel 18:20, 27-28; 1 Samuel 19:11-17; 1 Samuel 25:44; 2 Samuel 3; 2 Samuel 6:16-23; 1 Chronicles 15:29

9. Who was Michal?

10. How did she feel about David?

11. How did she come to be David's wife? (1 Sam.18:21, 28-29)

12. What did she refuse to do for her father? (1 Sam. 19:11-17)

13. What did Saul do with Michal while David was away? (1 Sam. 25:44; 2 Sam. 3:15-16)

14. Read 2 Samuel 6:16-23 and 1 Chronicles 15:29. How did Michal respond to the return of the Ark of the Covenant and David's celebration of it?

15. What do you think was wrong with her attitude?

16. What does Solomon say about the "contentious woman" in Proverbs 21:19 and 27:15?

Bathsheba

Scripture References: 2 Samuel 11, 12; 1 Kings 1:11-31; 1 Kings 2; Song of Solomon 3:11

This is a story you need to cover with your mother, rather than in class, due to the content of the story. There are, however, some things we can learn from the overall story, as a group.

16. Bathsheba becomes David's wife through a sweet courtship story.   TRUE or FALSE

17. Did David have Bathsheba's best interest at heart?   Explain your answer.

18. What does Bathsheba lose because of the sin involved in her relationship with David? (Two answers)

19. Who is her second son?

20. Does she look out for his interests until he is King?

Abigail

Scripture References: 1 Samuel 25; 1 Samuel 27:3; 1 Samuel 30:5; 2 Samuel 2:2; 2 Samuel 3:3; 1 Chronicles 3:1

21. Who is Abigail?

22. What does "Nabal" mean?

23. How is Abigail described in 1 Samuel 25:3?

24. How does Abigail handle the situation she walks into?

25. How does David respond? (1 Samuel 25:32-35)

26. To whom did David attribute Abigail's actions? (1 Samuel 25:39)

27. How did Abigail respond to David's proposal to become his wife?

All four of these women are examples of women in difficult relationships. Hannah and Michal had to deal with polygamous marriages. This added extra personalities and drama that each woman had to deal with in one way or another, I'm sure. We see it mainly in Hannah. Despite the abuses from Peninnah, Hannah didn't retaliate. Her behavior is different than that of Rachel and Leah! She shows that faith will get you through, and that you never give up talking to God about your hurts.

Michal, Abigail and Bathsheba show what can happen when your life is connected with someone who does not have your best interest at heart. You can learn to be aware of the signs that someone is looking out for their own interests only rather than trying to protect you.

Abigail shows courage under fire, submission to a hard man, and quick thinking! Notice that the FIRST thing mentioned of her is that she is INTELLIGENT. She doesn't make excuses for Nabal. She doesn't wail and cry at David to get him to reconsider. She takes care of what David had a right to expect from any of his people, and reminds him that he has a greater moment than this one indignation from Nabal coming when he becomes king. David so recognized her exceptional qualities that he wanted her to be his wife after Nabal died.

So learn from these women, be diligent to lean on God like Hannah and learn the wisdom that can give you grace in difficult circumstances like Abigail. Learn from Michal and Bathsheba's unfortunate situations and avoid the same.

Philippians 2:4 "Let each of you look out not only for his own interests, but also for the interests of others."

Proverb 3:5 "Trust in the Lord with all your heart and do not lean on your own understanding."

Study Builders

Use this page to note all the verses from the lesson into one or more of the categories.

In Manner of Life In Purity	In Word
In Love	In Faith

Additional Notes:

Lesson 15

Friendship

1. Look up, and then write, a definition of "friend" here.

2. What does Luke 15:9 say friends do together?

3. How is the friend described in Deuteronomy 13:6?

4. Read 1 Samuel 18:1, 3. David and Saul's son Jonathan were not very good friends.

TRUE or FALSE

5. What is said of Abraham in James 2:23?

6. Use your concordance to locate the Old Testament verse to which James 2:23 may be referring.

7. In what way(s) can Ecclesiastes 4:9-12 apply to friendship?

8. What did Job's friends do for him? (Job 2:11-13)

9. Write Proverb 12:26 here.

10. A friend is someone you expect to be able to trust. (Psalm 41:9)   TRUE or FALSE

11. Fill in the blanks. Proverb 17:17

     A friend _____ loves at all _____, and a brother is _____ for
_____.

12. People should be our friends even if we aren't friendly towards them. (Proverb
18:24)   TRUE or FALSE

13. Who did Jesus say were His friends? (John 15:14)

14. What kind of friend is Jesus? (John 15:13)

15. What does a friend's "hearty counsel" do? (Proverb 27:9)

16. Fill in the blanks. Proverb 119:63

     "I am a _____ of all who _____ You, and of those who _____ Your
precepts."

17. According to 1 Peter 1:22, how are we to love one another?

18. How did the Lord speak to Moses, in Exodus 33:11?

19. Friends always give the right advice. (Esther 5:14; Deut. 13:6; Job 42:7)

          TRUE or FALSE

20. Explain Proverb 19:6 in your own words.

21. How did the Shulammite describe the Shepherd? (Song of Solomon 5:16)

22. Research – use your concordance to find more references about friends. You can search for "companion" as well.

After you've found and READ all the verses, write a short paragraph that covers all the situations dealt with in the scriptures. Can you think of any situation that isn't covered?

Friendship is a blessing from the Lord. As we can see from the multitude of verses on the subject, God approves of friendship! He doesn't expect you to walk through this life all alone. He created you and knows your needs. Just as Adam couldn't find a companion suitable among the animals, we too need other humans to balance out our lives. As always, God is thorough. We need to be CAREFUL about who we have as our friends. Not just casual acquaintances that you might have coffee with on occasion; the friends who you take into your confidence, who are as your own "soul" as Jonathan and David were to one another. These people WILL influence you – it's not a matter of maybe they will, they WILL influence you. HOW they influence you is up to what you allow into your life. We're back to CHOICES. Realize that friendship is worth the work that you put into it. You MUST put something into it yourself, or it's not a true friendship. Anything worth having is worth fighting for AND waiting for. Be God's friend FIRST, as Abraham and Moses were, then make your friends from the people around you who are friends of God. Always being on guard to protect your soul and to be ready to protect theirs if need be.

Study Builders

Use this page to note all the verses from the lesson into one or more of the categories.

In Manner of Life In Purity	*In Word*
In Love	*In Faith*

Additional Notes:

Lesson 16

Serving Others

Have you noticed yet that everything in your life is NOT all about you AND is all about you? I know that sounds contradictory. We've been created so that we might bring glory to God (Eccl. 12:13; 1 Peter 4:16). It is often said that the Bible is the story of Jesus: Jesus is coming, Jesus is here, Jesus is coming again. So it's really all about Him. BUT – it's also all about HOW YOU RESPOND TO HIM. So, it's not all about what you want, like, or need. It's about you doing what God wants, likes, and needs. You are a part of it when you put on Christ in baptism. So let's talk about your part towards OTHERS.

Read John 13:34-35.

1. What is the "new" commandment given in verse 34?

2. What will obeying this command tell others about you?

3. Write Galatians 5:13 here.

Read Ephesians 4 - 5:21.

4. How does Paul tell us to go about walking "worthy of the calling with which you were called"? (Eph.4:1-3)

5. For what purpose did Christ give some to be "apostles, some prophets, some evangelists, and some pastors and teachers"? (Eph. 4:11-13)

6. Having others to equip and edify us protects us from what in Eph. 4:14?

7. What is the end result of brethren following these commands? (Eph. 4:15-16)

8. Why should we put away lying, according to Ephesians 4:25?

9. Why should the thief steal no more but work with his hands? (Eph. 4:28)

10. Why watch what you say, according to Ephesians 4:29?

11. I should put away the things in Ephesians 4:31-32 only because my life will be better for it.   TRUE or FALSE

12. How are we to walk? (Eph. 5:2)

13. We are to have "no fellowship" with what? (Eph. 5:11)

Fellowship is to be connected to something or someone, associated with, in agreement. Remember our lesson on friends? Again we see that we need to CHOOSE our relationships carefully.

14. List all the things that fall into walking "circumspectly" from Eph. 5:15-21.

     a.

     b.

     c.

     d.

     e.

     f.

     g.

     h.

15. The consolation in Christ is found only when we serve God without any regard for others. (Phil. 2:1-4)   TRUE or FALSE

16. Who are we imitating when we look out for each other? (Phil. 2:5)

17. How is a woman "qualified" to be a widow that can be supported by the church? (1Timothy 5:9, 10)

18. Write 1 Peter 5:5 here.

19. How are we to "honor" in Romans 12:10?

20. What does Romans 12:3 tell us?

Read John 13:1-20. This is our ultimate example of service. Jesus teaches His apostles about true leadership and love toward your fellow man. The lesson is given by Jesus' washing the apostles' feet.

21. Fill in the blanks. John 13:1.

    "Now before the feast of the Passover, when Jesus knew that His hour had come that He should _____ from this world to the _____, having _____ His _____ who were in the world, He _____ them to the _____."

22. What does Jesus tell them the point is in John 13:14-15?

You were not put on this Earth to be done for, but rather to learn to do for others. As we've seen, this is how people KNOW you BELONG to Christ! So you may ask, "what about me, what can I do?" What can you do? Are there not people around you who could use your help? Start at home, being a helper. Most likely your mother has been training you to do this already. Take it to heart, thank her for making the way easier for you, and start to WORK with a THANKFUL HEART that you have a way to SERVE! There are many ways you can do for others, not the least of which is to PRAY for them (James 5:16). As you go through your week, think about ways you might be able to help others.

In Your Bible –

Colossians 3-4:9 and Galatians 5:16-6:10

Study Builders

Use this page to note all the verses from the lesson into one or more of the categories.

In Manner of Life In Purity	In Word
In Love	In Faith

Additional Notes:

Lesson 17

Listening to God

By this point in the study, I hope that you are already hearing God through the scriptures that we've been reading. We've covered many topics, and there should be no doubt that God has instructed you. But are you REALLY listening? Are you taking these things in and allowing them to become part of who you are? Maybe you feel that to have the knowledge is enough? Maybe you think "that's all well and good, but I'll just do what I can and not worry about the rest"? Every one of us needs to realize that God's word only works when we allow it to WORK in our LIVES (Phil. 1:6; Phil. 2:12-13). So, let's see what we can see what benefits come from listening to God to the point of OBEDIENCE.

Back to Psalm 1:1-4.

1. What does verse 2 say about the man who does not walk in the counsel of the ungodly?

2. Define "delight" using a concordance or lexicon.

Read Galatians 5:22-23.

3. What does Paul mean by "fruit"?

4. List the fruit of the Spirit. (9 things)

5. The Spirit gives us what? (John 6:63; Eph.6:17)

6. What will God do for those who hope in Him? (Ps.31:24)

7. We shouldn't expect our faith to grow very much as we learn. (Col.2:6-7)

       TRUE or FALSE

8. What can God do for the weak and weary? (Isaiah 40:27-31)

9. In Deut. 4:1, what reason does Moses give to Israel for listening to God?

10. What will God do if you acknowledge Him in all your ways? (Prov. 3:5-6)

11. What did David ask for in Psalm 25:4-5?

12. What comes to those who trust in the Lord? (Psalm 32:10-11)

13. Write Isaiah 48:17 here.

WOW! Wouldn't we be FOOLISH to ignore ALL of what God has told us? The blessings that come from our listening to Him AND doing what He says are endless!

14. Think about some of the people God has told us about:

Daniel – would Daniel have done well if he had not listened to God and obeyed Him?

Joseph (Genesis 37-50) – Would Joseph have been of any help to his family if he had not been faithful to God while he was in Egypt and away from his family?

What about Noah, Esther, David, Ruth, and all the others we read of in scripture who followed God? Can you see how any of them would have been saved or applauded if they'd been different than they were?

Abraham – a man hears a voice that tells him to move his family to a place he does not know. He recognized the voice of God and obeyed! We can follow that example!

15. What statement is made in 1 Peter 3:12-14 about those who follow "good"?

16. What did Jesus leave with us, through His apostles? (John 14:27)

17. Read Romans 8:37-39. What can separate you from the love of God while you walk in it?

18. What comes from "hearing" in Romans 10:17 and John 5:24?

19. What brings everlasting life and saves, according to John 3:36 and Mark 16:16?

20. Why does God command men to repent? (Acts 17:30-31; Acts 2:38)

21. What is hearing connected to in Acts 18:8?

22. What confession is connected with salvation? (Matthew 10:32-33; Romans 10:9-10)

23. What is baptism connected to in Romans 6:3 and Colossians 2:12?

24. To whom is Christ the author of eternal salvation? (Hebrews 5:9)

Conclusion:

Now, which of those things do you want to miss because you're not interested in "listening" right now?

God has blessed you with so much! We haven't touched on all of His provisions for us here, not by a long shot. I hope that you can see that to listen to Him is COMFORT and PROTECTION. To listen to God is the most sensible thing to do. He doesn't expect immediate perfect results from you. He knows that your faith is a growing process. Fortunately, He's given you a recipe for success!

2 Peter 1:2-11

"Grace and peace be multiplied to you in the knowledge of God and of Jesus our Lord."

For the reason of having escaped the corruption that is in the world GIVE ALL DILIGENCE

Add to FAITH VIRTUE

Add to virtue KNOWLEDGE

Add to knowledge SELF-CONTROL

Add to self-control PERSEVERANCE

Add to perseverance GODLINESS

Add to godliness BROTHERLY KINDNESS

ADD to brotherly kindness LOVE

IF these are yours and ABOUND you will be neither barren nor unfruitful in the knowledge of our Lord Jesus Christ.

He who LACKS these things is SHORTSIGHTED, even to BLINDNESS, and has FORGOTTEN that he was cleansed for his old sins.

IF you DO these things you will never STUMBLE; for so an entrance will be SUPPLIED to you ABUNDANTLY into the EVERLASTING KINGDOM!

What a PROMISE! Peter and John chose to LISTEN to God (Acts 4:19). Won't you do the same?

"but GROW in the grace and knowledge of our Lord and Savior Jesus Christ. To Him be the glory both now and forever. Amen." 2Peter 3:18 (emphasis mine, ADL)

Study Builders

Use this page to note all the verses from the lesson into one or more of the categories.

In Manner of Life In Purity	In Word
In Love	**In Faith**

Additional Notes:

Lesson 18

All Things are Possible

Real life situation: Someone comes and says "I've got a job for you." Possible responses: "Who am I that you'd ask me to do something that important?" "What if they don't believe me that my orders are from the boss?" "What if the others won't listen to me?" "I'm really not very good at that kind of thing." "Can't you just send someone else?" (All these were said by Moses in Exodus 3 and 4.)

Are you ever like this? Do you question your ability to do something? How do you respond to new challenges?

What about your dreams? Do you believe they won't come to be for one reason or another? Do you hope one kind of life for yourself, but expect quite another?

How do you see yourself right NOW? How much do you think you bring to the table of "just getting through" in this life?

Read Jeremiah 29:10-14.

1. What thoughts did God have toward Israel/Judah?

2. What did God promise He would do when they "call upon Me and go and pray to Me"?

Ok, that's Israel, what about us today?

3. Read Matthew 7:7-8. What is the promise given here?

The apostles believed that Jesus' teaching made it impossible for people to get to heaven – the rules were just too strict.

4. What was Jesus' response in Matthew 19:26?

Heaven is a glorious reward! But it takes sacrifice in this life to accomplish God's will and attain to be there. (Matthew 19:29-30). We can't hold anything higher than our service to the Lord.

Read Philippians 4:12-13.

5. What are the "all things" that Paul is talking about in verse 13?

Read Matthew 13:31-32.

6. Mustard seed is an herb that grows into a _____.

Read Matthew 17:20

7. How much faith does it take to move mountains?

Read Matthew 21:20-22.

8. What promise is made here and what condition is put upon it?

Read Psalm 34:11-16.

9. What is the way to have "life" and "many days"?

10. In Psalm 34:17-18, does God know about your broken heart?

11. What does God promise in Matthew 6:33-34?

Are you impressed yet? Do you realize that you can do ANYTHING if God is with you? If not, just hold on!

Read Ephesians 3:14-21.

12. What will we be able to comprehend with all the saints? (verse 18)

13. Verse 19 says we will know the love of Christ which _____ _____.

14. What is left out of verses 20-21 that Jesus can't do?

15. What works in us?

16. What is that "power" according to Romans 1:16-17?

Read Philippians 1:3-6.

17. Who had begun a "good work" in the brethren in Philippi?

18. Who would finish the work?

19. How can we apply these verses to ourselves individually?

20. What does 2 Timothy 2:15 say we should do as workers for God?

21. What is the promise of Matthew 6:33-34?

Conclusion:

When we talked about serving others we discussed not thinking more highly of ourselves than we ought (Romans 12:3). Humility is a difficult thing to hold on to. The "than you ought" part means there is a level at which you should think of yourself – you just shouldn't exceed it! We began this study learning just how much God values us. We need to remember that! When you begin to feel down on yourself because things aren't going the way they should be (or the way you think they should be) – remember that God loves you, holds you up, and will make a way (John 16:27; Psalm 63:8; 1 Cor. 10:13).

He is POWERFUL! He can do all things. He's promised His help to us. So we should feel empowered to move mountains BY HIS WILL. Recognize your gifts – what you are able to do. Not everyone can do all things well. We're not meant to! We're meant to do OUR part, so others can do theirs without needing to fill a gap we've left open.

Don't be like Moses, making excuses and trying to get out of God's work for Him. Instead, be like Moses, who went forward with God's help and saved a nation! Don't reduce God's creation of you to something worthless by saying you have no part to play. Rather, hold your head high as a child of God, confident that He is standing right beside you, and step into the role that is waiting for you. Imitate Paul and say that whatever comes, you can "do all things through Christ who strengthens me."

Study Builders

Use this page to note all the verses from the lesson into one or more of the categories.

In Manner of Life In Purity	In Word
In Love	In Faith

Additional Notes:

Lesson 19

Two Chosen Mothers – Elizabeth and Mary

Elizabeth

Scripture References – Luke 1:5-25, 36-37, 39-45, 57-80.

1. Who is Elizabeth?

2. How is she described in Luke 1:6-7?

3. Her husband went away to spend his time working in the Temple as a priest, how was he when he came home? (Luke 1:23)

4. How did Elizabeth respond when she realized she was having a baby?

5. What does the angel Gabriel say to Mary about Elizabeth in Luke 1:36-37?

6. Who visited Elizabeth when she was six months pregnant?

7. Tell what happened during this visit.

8. When it was time for Elizabeth to have her baby, how did her neighbors and relatives react?

9. Read Luke 1:59-60. What does Elizabeth's statement show she understood?

10. Verse 80 says "the child grew and became strong in the spirit," what part do you think Elizabeth played in this?

<u>Mary</u>

Scripture References – Matthew 1:18-25; 2:11, 13-15, 19-23; 13:55-56; Mark 6:3; Luke 1:26-56: Luke 2; John 19:25; Acts 1:14

11. Write Isaiah 7:14 here.

Read Luke 1:26-56.

12. Who did the angel go to see in Nazareth?

13. How does the angel greet her?

14. What was Mary's response?

15. What is said of her in verse 30?

16. Can you think of another Bible character of whom something similar is said? (hint, I'm thinking about the book of Genesis and lots of water. ☺)

17. What is Mary being called to do? (verses 31-33)

18. Mary naturally questions how this will all happen. How does the angel Gabriel reassure her that it is true and possible? (verses 36-37)

19. How does Mary respond when her questions have been answered? (verse 38)

20. How does the Holy Spirit, speaking through Elizabeth, describe Mary? (verses 41-45)

21. Why were these things happening to Mary? (Luke 1:45; Matthew 1:22-23)

23. Luke records for us a song that Mary spoke about these events.

What does Mary tell us in this song? Make a list of things. (i.e. v.48 God noticed her even though she is spiritually unfit for His notice.)

1.
2.
3.
4.
5.
6.
7.
8.
9.
10.

24. Read verse 49, for whom does she say God did these things?

25. Write, in a short paragraph, the story of Jesus' birth from Luke 2:1-20.

26. Mary was worshipped as well as Jesus after He was born. (Matthew 2:11)
                    TRUE or FALSE

27. How did Mary respond to the visit from the shepherds and the spreading of the news of her Son's birth? (Luke 2:19)

28. What does the visit to Jerusalem when Jesus is 8 days old tell us about His earthly parents? (Luke 2:22-27, 39)

30. How did Joseph and Mary react to Simeon's prophecy? (Luke 2:33)

31. Was this life journey going to be an easy one for Mary? (Luke 2:34-35)

32. How did Mary respond to finding Jesus in the Temple after thinking He was lost? (Luke 2:48-50)

33. What did Mary do after the incident in the Temple? (Luke 2:51)

34. Did Mary have any other children? (Matthew 13:55-56)

35. Where was Mary when her Son was on the cross? (John 19:25-27)

36. Where was Mary after Jesus ascended to Heaven? (Acts 1:14)

Conclusion:

These two women are at opposite ends of the stages of the adult time of life: Mary is young and unmarried, while Elizabeth is older, married for many years, and past child bearing. Yet both have their devotion to the Lord noted in Scripture! What worthy examples for each one of us to strive to imitate – no matter which stage of life we are in ourselves. Worshipping God is not a YOUNG thing, nor is it reserved for the OLDER. Living a FULL life in SERVICE to Him is always something we can achieve. We simply have to set our minds to it. Mary and Joseph went to Jerusalem as the customs of the law dictated. This took preparation to pull off. It was not a simple, last minute trip – as is seen when they make the trip when she is 9 months pregnant! Both women were called Blessed because of God's choosing them for motherhood. They weren't saints, just women – but what WONDERFUL WOMEN. I pray that every young lady would strive to be like Mary, and I pray that every woman strive to be like Elizabeth. Don't dismiss your "timeliness" to serve due to your youth or being older. God has work for ALL of you!

Study Builders

Use this page to note all the verses from the lesson into one or more of the categories.

In Manner of Life In Purity	In Word
In Love	In Faith

Additional Notes:

Lesson 20

Lessons from Anna; Mary and Martha

Anna

Scripture Reference – Luke 2:36-38

1. Describe Anna.

2. How often did Anna serve God?

3. What did she do after seeing Jesus with His parents at the Temple?

4. Consider 1 Timothy 5:11-16. How does Paul tell Timothy to instruct the young widows?

Young people need FOCUS to keep their lives on track. Older people do as well, but the implication is that if you have done these things when you are young, then they are more likely to be an ingrained HABIT and part of LIFE when you are older. Anna is an example of a VERY DEDICATED woman. Strive to be this DEDICATED in whatever manner you SERVE the Lord and others.

Mary and Martha

Scripture References – Luke 10:38-42; John 11:1-44; Matthew 26:6-13; John 12:1-8

5. Who welcomed Jesus into her house? (Luke 10:38)

6. Who are her siblings? (Give references to prove.)

7. What is said of Martha in Luke 10:40?

8. What was Mary doing?

9. What did Jesus say to Martha?

10. We should always leave the serving to others while we do that which interests us.

TRUE or FALSE

Read John 11:1-44.

11. What did the sisters do when Lazarus became ill? (verse 3)

12. How did they refer to Lazarus in their message?

13. How did Jesus feel about Martha, Mary, and Lazarus?

14. How long did Jesus wait to go to Bethany, and why? (verses 4, 6, 12)

15. How far away from Jerusalem was Bethany?

16. How long had Lazarus been dead when Jesus got to Bethany?

17. What did both Martha and Mary believe would have happened if Jesus had come sooner? (verse 21, 32)

18. What does Martha believe can happen now? (verse 22)

19. What confession does Martha make in verse 27?

20. Martha fully understood that Jesus was "the resurrection". (John 11:25-27; 39-42)

NOTE: As an aside to our study – notice how much Jesus cared for these people! He's already said that He's going to wake Lazarus up, so He knows there isn't going to be a reason to be sad (John 11:11). Yet He still weeps over the mourning of Mary and Martha AND at the death of Lazarus. This Lord TRULY knows what pains each of us go through in this life (Hebrews 2:17-18; 4:14-16).

21. When Jesus returns to Bethany before the Passover, where does He go? (John 12:1)

22. What did Mary and Martha do during this visit?

23. What did Jesus say about Mary's service? (John 12:7)

Conclusion:

 Martha and Mary were BUSY! Martha and Mary befriended Jesus when He had nowhere to call home. Martha could get distracted with the work around the house. Mary could be distracted by her grief so as not to notice the absence of her sister. Both of these women show a deep belief in Jesus and WHO He is. Both of these women show an eagerness to serve. Each woman has her talents. They each did what they could when they could. They weren't the SAME, but they both SERVED.

We can each try to be more like Anna, Mary, and Martha. We can each dedicate ourselves to God with our own abilities at the stage of life that we are in now. We don't have to wait until we are of "great age" to know what we can do for the Lord and for others. We need to be thankful for the abilities that others bring to the table, and grateful for the opportunity to share our own.

Study Builders

Use this page to note all the verses from the lesson into one or more of the categories.

In Manner of Life In Purity	In Word
In Love	In Faith

Additional Notes:

Lesson 21

Women of the Lord's church

(Eunice and Lois, Euodia and Syntyche, Sapphira, Priscilla, and Lydia)

Sapphira

Acts4:32-37- 5:11

1. What were all of the people in the church doing in this context?

2. What did Ananias and Sapphira do? (Acts 5:1)

3. How much did they say they were giving? (implied from verses 4, 8)

4. Sapphira didn't have a choice because a wife must always obey her husband.

       TRUE or FALSE

Lesson learned – even those closest to you can lead you astray! You must know what is right and hold to it, no matter what those around you are doing. You will answer for the things that you do.

Lydia

Acts 16:11-15

5. Who were meeting to pray by the river in Philippi? (verse 13)

6. Who was Lydia?

7. How did she respond to the things she heard from Paul?

8. Lydia hesitated to share her home with her brethren.   TRUE or FALSE

9. See what you can find out about being a "seller of purple". Write a short paragraph about what this might tell us about Lydia.

Priscilla

Acts 18:1-3, 24-28; Romans 16:3; 1 Corinthians 16:19; 2 Timothy 4:19

10. Who is Priscilla?

11. What did she do for a living, along with her husband? (Acts 18:3)

12. Who took Apollos aside to teach him "more accurately" the way of God? (Acts 18:24-26)

13. Aquila and Priscilla only opened their home to Paul. (1 Cor. 16:19)

                    TRUE or FALSE

Note 2 Timothy 4:19, "Prisca and Aquila". Often name order has some significance. Back in Acts 12:25 it says "Barnabas and Saul" returned from Jerusalem. Then in Acts 13:43 we see "Paul and Barnabas". The name order goes along with who is in the lead, or more prominent in the events that are going on. Priscilla and Aquila are equally of help and given recommendation by Paul.

Euodia and Syntyche

Philippians 4:2, 3

14. What are Euodia and Syntyche having difficulty doing?

15. How does Paul describe them in verse 3?

16. What does Paul ask the brethren in Philippi to do for these women?

Even good, strong Christians have trouble getting along sometimes. We are human. It takes other loving, strong Christian FRIENDS to help get us back on track sometimes.

Eunice and Lois

Acts 16:1; 2 Tim.1:5

17. What do we learn about Eunice in Acts 16:1?

18. How is Lois described in 2 Timothy 1:5?

19. Parents and grandparents don't have much influence over the children in their lives.   TRUE or FALSE

Conclusion:

Women have always been a part of the Lord's church. It's not a fraternity. The world would have us believe that God, and Paul, don't appreciate women; don't notice women, and push women aside in favor of men, as we've discussed before. These women show Galatians 3:28-29 to be TRUE!

> "There is neither Jew nor Greek, there is neither slave nor free, there is neither male nor female; for you are all one in Christ Jesus. And if you are Christ's, then you are Abraham's seed, and heirs according to the promise."

Women have roles to fulfill, as do men. They may not be the same roles, but they are all of equal value to God. We can't all be preachers and elders (Ephesians 4:11-12). Not all of us are equally good at exhorting or showing mercy (Romans 12:6-8). We are all important in the things which we do. Strive to be a worker who is commended as Priscilla, Euodia, Syntyche, Lois, and Eunice were.   Avoid making the mistake of Sapphira of trying to be something that you are not and lying about it. Always be eager to learn and to make changes in your life like Lydia. Don't forget to THANK GOD for the examples He has laid out for you. These women are given in scripture to HELP you. Let them.

Study Builders

Use this page to note all the verses from the lesson into one or more of the categories.

In Manner of Life In Purity	In Word
In Love	**In Faith**

Additional Notes:

Lesson 22

The Woman in Proverbs 31 and the Widow in 1 Timothy 5

Depending upon your age, you may be wondering just how you are going to learn anything from these two women. They are not teenagers. They are not single. You may not be in their exact circumstance, but you can still learn from these women. Never underestimate the value of having something for which to STRIVE!

The Virtuous Wife in Proverbs 31:10-31

1. According to Proverbs 31:1, who is telling us about this woman?

2. Write Proverb 31:10 here.

3. What does "virtuous" mean?

4. This woman is a "jack of all trades", as they say. Make a list of all the things she does.

    a.

    b.

    c.

    d.

    e.

    f.

    g.

    h.

    i.

    j.

    k.

l.

m.

n.

o.

5. Explain verse 25.

6. Write verse 30 here.

7. Can you find another verse that compliments Proverbs 31:30?

The Widow in 1 Timothy 5:3-10

8. What does it mean to be a widow who is "really" a widow?

9. Who should be a widow's first source of comfort and support when she loses her husband?

10. List the qualifications for a widow, who is alone, to be able to be supported financially by the local church. (verses 5, 10)

a.

b.

c.

d.

e.

f.

g.

h.

i.

j.

11. The church can take care of any woman who has ever lost a husband. (verse 9, 11, and 16)   TRUE or FALSE

Conclusion:

Well, those are two very serious examples to follow! Did you notice something about both of them? I will give you a hint; it is the SAME thing we noticed about Mary and Martha, Anna, and Elizabeth. These two women are BUSY!

Compare Proverb 31:27 and 1 Timothy 5:13:

	(regarding the young widows)
"She watches over the ways of her household, and does not eat the bread of idleness."	..."they learn to be idle, wandering about from house to house, and not only idle but also gossips and busybodies, saying things which they ought not."

Proverb 31:27 describes the virtuous woman and the worthy widow! Notice that in 1 Timothy 5 it is the younger widows who have a tendency to misuse their time and talents. This does not mean that an older woman will not become a gossip. It just means that a younger woman is more LIKELY to do so.

So, what CAN you learn for the here and now? The main thing is to realize that these two women didn't happen overnight! They didn't say "I do" and become good housekeepers, loving wives, and caretakers of the needy and sick. They were these things, to one degree or another, BEFORE they were "married women". There are some things that you just can't do until you are older and married: being a mother and being a wife are the two obvious ones. Whether young or old you can be a helper of the needy – you just need to look for opportunities. You need to ASK what you can do, where you are needed. Begin by LEARNING how to teach a Bible class. You certainly can't teach one until you have learned how! Study your Bible to increase your knowledge so that you already have some when it comes time to learn how to share it with others. Learn to cook. You can't get meals to people who are ill if you can't make the meal. Start at the beginning and don't begrudge the journey! The character of these women built reputations that people could count on. You CAN do the same. All you need do is put your focus on WORKING for the Lord, as these women did. Do that and you WILL be a fruitful "worker for the Lord"!

Study Builders

Use this page to note all the verses from the lesson into one or more of the categories.

In Manner of Life In Purity	In Word
In Love	In Faith

Additional Notes:

Song of Solomon

These lessons are laid out a bit different from our previous lessons. Song of Solomon is a beautiful love story. As with ALL love stories, there are some parts that are not appropriate for discussion in groups that include younger people. It's not that it is WRONG, but that it is immodest (not to be left uncovered) and just not what a person not yet ready for marriage needs to be thinking about, in my opinion. There is a time and a place for all things. Some want young people to know about these things before they get to the age that they might happen to them – so the information for a full study is in this book. There is additional information provided in the Appendix.

As a recommendation, I suggest, in class that includes girls under the age of 16, that the teacher only hit the highlights. Reading through the whole book together (with minimal discussion) so the student can hear the beauty of the story as a whole and then discussing some of the general things to glean from the story.

These lessons have a copy of the book of Song of Solomon typed out without the normal headings that are usually found from various editors of printed Bibles. It has been broken up so that it reads as a play, or script, would.

I (the author) have put who I believe the speakers to be to one side, (We must try to understand who is talking), and only separated the story by the possible setting of the scenes. You may hear it differently than I do. Great! Talk about it, share it, and study it – all to try to understand God's word better.

So, let's get into this wonderful book!

Mrs. Angela Legg

1. Whose song is this? (S of S 1:1)

2. Write Ephesians 5:17 here.

God put this book into the Bible. He inspired its writing. Let's see what we can do to understand what we can from it, but not take more than is said.

(I've broken this down in the way in which I understand it best. I hope that it is beneficial to you. This is taken from the NKJV.)

The Song of Songs, which is Solomon's

(PART ONE, SCENE ONE – SETTING: THE ROYAL TENTS IN ISSACHAR 1:2-3:5)

SHULAMITE   Let Him kiss me with the

kisses of his mouth –

For your love is better than

wine,

Because of the fragrance of your good ointments.

Your name is ointment poured forth;

Therefore the virgins love you.

Draw me away!

(In the NASB it reads "Draw me after you, let us run together!" The NLT, NIV, ESV, and RSV are similar. This would then be the SHULAMITE without comment from the DAUGHTERS OF JERUSALEM.)

DAUGHTERS OF JERUSALEM

We will run after you.

SHULAMITE

The king has brought me into his

chambers.

DAUGHTERS OF JERUSALEM

We will be glad and rejoice in you.

We will remember your love more

than wine.

SHULAMITE (of the Beloved)

Rightly do they love you.

SHULAMITE

I am dark,

DAUGHTERS OF JERUSALEM   (interjecting)

but lovely,

SHULAMITE

O daughters of Jerusalem,

Like the tents of Kedar,

Like the curtains of Solomon.

Do not look upon me,

Because I am dark,

Because the sun has tanned

me.

My mother's sons were angry with

me:

They made me the keeper of

the vineyards,

But my own vineyard I have

not kept.

Tell me, O you whom I love,

Where do you feed you

flock,

Where do you make it rest at

noon?

For why should I be as one

who veils

herself by the flocks of

your companions?

DAUGHTERS OF JERUSALEM

If you do not know, O fairest

among women,

Follow in the footsteps of the flock,

And feed your little goats

Beside the shepherds' tents.

(PART ONE, SCENE TWO)

SOLOMON

I have compared you, my

love,

To my filly among Pharaoh's

chariots.

Your cheeks are lovely with

ornaments,

Your neck with chains of

gold.

DAUGHTERS OF JERUSALEM

We will make you ornaments

of gold

with studs of silver!

SHULAMITE

While the king is at his table,

my spikenard sends

forth its fragrance.

A bundle of myrrh is my

beloved to

me,

That lies all night between my

breasts.

My beloved is to me

a cluster of henna

blooms

in the vineyards of

En Gedi.

SOLOMON

Behold, you are fair, my love!

Behold, you are fair!

You have dove's eyes.

SHULAMITE

(THINKING OF HER BELOVED)

Behold you are handsome my
beloved!
Yes, pleasant!
Also our bed is green,
The beams of our houses are
cedar,
And our rafters of fir.

(she speaks out loud)

I am the Rose of Sharon,
And the lily of the valleys.

SOLOMON

Like a lily among thorns,
So is my love among the
daughters.

SHULAMITE

(THINKING OF HER BELOVED)

Like an apple tree among the trees
of the woods,
So is my Beloved among the
sons.
I sat down in his shade with
great delight,
And his fruit was sweet to my
taste.
He brought me to the banqueting
house,
And his banner over me was
love.

Sustain me with cakes of raisins,

Refresh me with apples,

For I am lovesick.

His left hand is under my head,

And his right hand embraces

me.

I charge you, O daughters of

Jerusalem,

By the gazelles or by the does of the

field,

Do not stir up nor awaken love until

it pleases!

(PART ONE, SCENE THREE)

SHULAMITE

The voice of my Beloved

Behold, he comes

leaping upon the mountains,

Skipping upon the hills.

My Beloved is like a gazelle

or a young stag.

Behold, he stands behind our

wall;

He is looking through the

windows,

Gazing through the lattice.

SHULAMITE

(RECOUNTING WORDS OF THE SHEPHERD)

My Beloved spoke, and said to me:

"Rise up, my love, my fair one,

and come away.

For lo, the winter is past,

the rain is over and gone.

The flowers appear on the

earth;

The time of singing has

come,

And the voice of the

turtledove

is heard in our land.

The fig tree puts forth her

green figs,

And the vines with the tender

grapes give a good

smell.

Rise up, my love, my fair one,

and come away!

O my dove, in the clefts of

the rock,

In the secret places of

the cliff,

Let me see your face,

Let me hear your voice;

For your voice is sweet,

And your face is

lovely."

(IN HER MEMORY, SHULAMITE TO THE SHEPHERD) Catch us the foxes!

The little foxes that

spoil the vines,

For our grapes have tender

grapes!

SHULAMITE

My Beloved is mine, and I

am his.

He feeds his flock among the

lilies.

Until the day breaks

And the shadows flee away

Turn, my Beloved,

And be like a gazelle
or a young stag

Upon the mountains of
Bether.

(PART ONE, SCENE FOUR)

SHULAMITE

By night on my bed I sought

the one I love;

(SHE TELLS OF A DREAM)

I sought him but I did not

find him.

"I will rise now," I said,

"and go about the city;

In the streets and in the

squares

I will seek the one I love."

I sought him, but I did not

find him.

The watchmen who go about

the city found me;

I said, "Have you seen the

one I love?"

Scarcely had I passed by

them,

When I found the one I love!

I held him and would not let

him go

Until I had brought him to

the house of my

mother

And into the chamber of her

who conceived me.

I charge you, O daughters of

Jerusalem,

By the gazelles or by the does

of the field,

Do not stir up nor awaken

love until it pleases!

(PART TWO – SETTING: ROYAL PROCESSION ENTERS JERUSALEM 3:6-11)

PEOPLE OF THE AREA

Who is this coming out of the

wilderness like pillars of

smoke,

(COULD BE ONE, OR SEVERAL SPEAKERS)

Perfumed with myrrh and

frankincense,

With all the merchants'

fragrant powders?

Behold, it is Solomon's couch,

With sixty valiant men around it, of

the valiant of Israel.

They all hold swords, being expert

in war.

Every man has his sword on

his thigh

because of fear in the night.

Of the wood of Lebanon Solomon

the King

made himself a palanquin:

He made its pillars of silver

Its support of gold,

Its seat of purple,

Its interior paved with love by the

daughters of Jerusalem.

Go forth, O daughters of Zion,

And see King Solomon with the

crown with which his mother

crowned him

On the day of his wedding,

the day of the gladness
of his heart.

Questions –

1. Write a phrase or sentence that shows that the Shulamite had a positive self-image.

(note the scripture reference as well, by matching it up in in your Bible)

2. The Shulamite is sitting at the King Solomon's table. Find verses elsewhere in scripture that describe the riches of Solomon's table.

3. Write Proverb 15:17 here.

4. Write Proverb 17:1 here.

5. Hebrews 13:4 says that marriage is _____.

6. The Shulamite was not sure that the Shepherd cared for her.   TRUE or FALSE

Use a scripture to prove your answer. _____

7. Solomon came out disguised like one of the local people.   TRUE or FALSE

   Use a verse to prove your answer. _____

(PART THREE, SCENE ONE – SETTING: IN THE ROYAL PALACE IN JERUSALEM 4:1-8:4)

SOLOMON

> Behold, you are fair, my love!
>
> Behold, you are fair!
>
> You have dove's eyes behind your veil.
>
> Your hair is like a flock of goats going down from Mount Gilead.
>
> Your teeth are like a flock of shorn Sheep which have come up from the washing,
>
> Every one of which bears twins, and none is barren among them.
>
> Your lips are like a strand of scarlet, and your mouth is lovely.
>
> Your temples behind your veil are like a piece of pomegranate.
>
> Your neck is like the tower of David,

built for an armory

on which hang a thousand

bucklers, all

shields of mighty men.

Your two breasts are like two fawns,

twins of a gazelle, which feed

among the lilies.

SHULAMITE   Until the day breaks and the shadows flee

away,

I will go my way to the mountain of

myrrh

and to the hill of

frankincense.

SHULAMITE   You are all fair, my love, and there is no

spot in you.

(REMEMBERING THE SHEPHERD'S WORDS)   Come with me from

Lebanon, my spouse,

with me from Lebanon.

Look from the top of Amana.

From the top of Senir and Hermon,

From the lions' dens,

From the mountains of the

leopards.

You have ravished my heart, my
sister, my spouse;
You have ravished my heart with
one look of your eyes,
With one link of your
necklace.
How fair is your love, my sister, my
spouse!
How much better than wine is your
love,
And the scent of your perfumes
than all spices!
Your lips, O my spouse, drip as the
honeycomb;
Honey and milk are under your
tongue;
And the fragrance of your garments
is like the fragrance of
Lebanon.
A garden enclosed is my sister, my
spouse,
A spring shut up, a fountain
sealed.
Your plants are an orchard of
pomegranates

                                        with pleasant fruits,
                                Fragrant henna with
                                        spikenard,
                                        spikenard and saffron,
                                Calamus and cinnamon,
                                With all trees of
                                        frankincense, myrrh
                                        and aloes,
                                With all the chief spices.
                                A fountain of gardens, a well
                                        of living waters and
                                        streams from Lebanon.

SHULAMITE   Awake, O north wind,
                                And come, O south!
                                Blow upon my garden that its spices
                                        may flow out.
                                Let my beloved come to his garden
                                        and eat its pleasant fruits.

SHULAMITE   I have come to my garden, my
                                        sister, my spouse;
(HOW SHE IMAGINES THE SHEPHERD I have gathered my myrrh
    WILL RESPOND)   with my spice;
                                I have eaten my honeycomb

with my honey;

I have drunk my wine with

my milk.

Eat, O friends!

Drink, yes, drink

deeply, O beloved ones!

THE BELOVED OR WEDDING GUESTS
(SHE CONTINUES HER REMEMBERING)

(PART THREE, SCENE TWO 5:2-6:3)

SHULAMITE

(SHE TELLS OF ANOTHER DREAM)

I sleep, but my heart is awake;

It is the voice of my beloved!

He knocks, saying,

"Open for me, my sister, my love,

my dove, my perfect one;

For my head is covered with dew,

my locks with the drops of

the night."

"I have taken off my robe,

how can I put it on

again?

I have washed my feet, how

can I defile them?

My beloved put his hand by the

latch of the door, and my

heart yearned for him.

I arose to open for my beloved, and

my hands dripped with

myrrh,

My fingers with liquid myrrh, on the

handles of the lock.

I opened for my beloved,

but my beloved had turned

away and was gone.

My heart leaped up when he spoke.

I sought him, but I could not find

him;

I called him, but he gave no answer.

The watchmen who went about the

city found me.

They struck me, they

wounded me;
The keepers of the walls took

my veil away from me.

SHULAMITE

I charge you, O daughters of

Jerusalem,

(TO DAUGHTERS OF JERUSALEM)

If you find my beloved, that you tell

him I am lovesick!

DAUGHTERS OF JERUSALEM

What is your beloved more than

another beloved,

O fairest among women?

What is your beloved more than

another beloved that you so

charge us?

SHULAMITE

My beloved is white and ruddy,

chief among ten thousand.

His head is like the finest gold,

his locks are wavy and black

as a raven.

His eyes are like doves by the rivers

of waters, washed with milk,

and fitly set.

His cheeks are like a bed of spices,

banks of scented herbs.

His lips are lilies dripping liquid

myrrh.

His hands are rods of gold set with

beryl.

His body is carved ivory inlaid with

sapphires.

His legs are pillars of marble set on

bases of fine gold.

His countenance is like Lebanon,

excellent as the cedars.

His mouth is most sweet,

Yes, he is altogether lovely.

This is my beloved,

And this is my friend.

O daughters of

Jerusalem!

DAUGHTERS OF JERUSALEM

Where has your beloved gone, o

fairest among women?

Where has your beloved turned

aside, that we may seek him

with you?

SHULAMITE

My beloved has gone to his garden,

to the bed of spices, to feed

his flock in the gardens and

to gather lilies.

I am my beloved's and my beloved

is mine.

He feeds his flock among the lilies.

Questions –

1. Solomon knew the Shulamite well and was impressed with her good character.

TRUE or FALSE Use a verse to prove your answer. _____

2. The Shepherd knew the Shulamite well and was impressed with character.

TRUE or FALSE Use a verse to prove your answer. _____

3. How does Solomon describe the Shulamite? (4:1-5) You don't need to give details, explain the general idea.

4. How does the Shepherd describe the Shulamite? (4:7-15) You don't need to give details, explain the general idea.

5. The Shulamite's second dream comforted her.
    TRUE or FALSE

6. How does the Shulamite describe the Shepherd? (5:10-16)

7. The daughters of Jerusalem don't think the Shepherd sounds very nice.
    TRUE or FALSE

Lesson 25

Song of Solomon – part 3

Chapters 6:4 – 8:14

(PART THREE, SCENE THREE 6:4-8:4)

SOLOMON

O, my love, you are as beautiful as Tirzah,

Lovely as Jerusalem,

Awesome as an army with banners!

Turn your eyes away from me for they

have overcome me.

Your hair is like a flock of goats going

down from Gilead.

Your teeth are like a flock of sheep

which have come up from the

washing;

Every one bears twins, and none is

barren among them.

Like a piece of pomegranate are your

temples behind your veil.

There are sixty queens

and eighty concubines and virgins

wiithout number.

My dove, my perfect one, is the only one.

The only one of her mother;

The favorite of the one who bore
her.
The daughters saw her, and called her
"blessed".
The queens and the concubines, and they
praised her.
Who is she who looks forth as the
morning, fair as the moon, clear as
the sun,
Awesome as an army with banners?

SHULAMITE   I went down to the garden of nuts to see
the verdure of the valley;
To see whether the vine had
budded
and the pomegranates had
bloomed.
Before I was even aware,
my soul had made me as the
chariots of my noble people.

SOLOMON AND DAUGHTERS OF JERUSALEM   Return, return, O Shulamite:
Return, return, that we may look
upon you!

SHULAMITE   What would you see in the
Shulamite, as it were the

DAUGHTERS OF JERUSALEM

dance of the two camps?

How beautiful are your feet in

sandals,

O prince's daughter!

The curves of your thighs are

like jewels,

the work of the hands

of a skillful workman.

Your naval is a rounded goblet,

it lacks no blended beverage.

Your waist is a heap of wheat set

about with lilies.

Your two breasts are like two fawns,

twins of a gazelle.

Your neck is like an ivory tower.

Your eyes like the pools in

Heshbon by the gate of Bath

Rabbim.

Your nose is like the tower of

Lebanon which looks toward

Damascus.

Your head crowns you like Mount

Carmel and the hair of your

head is like purple.

A king is held captive by your

tresses!

SOLOMON

How fair and how pleasant you are,
O love, with your delights!
This stature of yours is like a
palm tree,
And your breasts like its
clusters.
I said, "I will go up to the palm tree,
I will take hold of its
branches."
Let now your breasts be like clusters
of the vine,
The fragrance of your breath like
apples,
And the roof of your mouth like the
best wine.

SHULAMITE

The wine goes down smoothly for my
beloved,
moving gently the lips of sleepers.
I am my beloved's, and his desire is
toward me.

(TO THE SHEPHERD)

Come, my beloved, let us go forth to the
field;
Let us lodge in the villages.

Let us get up early to the vineyards,

let us see if the vine has

budded.

Whether the grape blossoms are open,

and the pomegranates are in bloom.

There I will give you my love.

The mandrakes give off a fragrance,

and at our gates are pleasant fruits,

all manner, new and old,

Which I have laid up for you, my

beloved.

Oh, that you were like my brother, who

nursed at my mother's breasts!

If I should find you outside, I would

kiss you;

I would not be despised.

I would lead you and bring you into

the house of my mother,

She who used to instruct me.

I would cause you to drink of spiced

wine, of the juice of my

pomegranate.

(TO DAUGHTERS OF JERUSALEM)   His left hand is under my head, and

his right hand embraces me.

I charge you, O daughters of

Jerusalem,

do not stir up nor awaken

love until it pleases!

(PART FOUR, SCENE 1 – SETTING: IN ISSACHAR 8:5-14)

PEOPLE FROM THE COUNTRYSIDE   Who is this coming up from the

wilderness, leaning on her

beloved?

SHEPHERD   I awakened you under the apple

tree,

there your mother brought

you forth;

There she who bore you brought

you forth.

Set me as a seal upon your heart, as

a seal upon your arm;

for love is as strong as death.

Jealousy as cruel as the grave;

Its flames are flames of

fire, a most vehement

flame!

Many waters cannot quench love,

nor can the floods drown it.

If a man would give for love all the
wealth of his house,
it would be utterly despised.

WEDDING GUESTS

"We have a little sister, and she has
no breasts.
What shall we do for our sister in
the day when she is spoken
for?
If she is a wall, we will build upon
her a battlement of silver;
And if she is a door, we will enclose
her with boards of cedar."

SHULAMITE

I am a wall and my breasts like
towers;
Then I became in his eyes as one
who found peace.
Solomon had a vineyard at Baal
Hamon;
He leased the vineyard to keepers;
Everyone was to bring for its fruit
a thousand silver coins.
My own vineyard is before me.
You, O Solomon, may have a

thousand,

and those who tend its fruit

two hundred.

SHEPHERD

You who dwell in the gardens,

The companions listen for your

voice –

Let me hear it!

SHULAMITE

Make haste my beloved, and be like

a gazelle or a young stag on

the mountains of spices.

Questions –

1. Solomon has learned new things to love about the Shulamite, by this time.
TRUE or FALSE

2. Deep down, the daughters of Jerusalem are more like the Shulamite than they are Solomon.   TRUE or FALSE

3. What is the THEME of Song of Solomon? (give a verse)

4. The Shulamite had second thoughts about not marrying Solomon.
TRUE or FALSE

Study Builders

Use this page to note all the verses from the lesson into one or more of the categories.

In Manner of Life In Purity	In Word
In Love	In Faith

Additional Notes:

Lesson 26

A Look at Woman's All

You made it! We are at the end of our study. I hope that you are more confident about God's love for you. I hope that you have come to see that there is WORK that YOU can DO in God's Kingdom. God made Adam and Eve and said His creation was "very good" (Genesis 1:31). I want to take this last lesson to paint the full picture of what you are striving to become – a woman of God. We've looked at different aspects of womanhood through the study of this book. Here I hope we can tie it all together in one glorious bow.

Scripture References: Ecclesiastes 12; 1 Peter 2 and 3; 1 Timothy 2; Titus 2

Read Ecclesiastes 12:13-14.

1. What is the "conclusion of the whole matter"?

2. Who is the source of these teachings? (Eccl. 12:11)

3. Who does Solomon tell to "remember your Creator" in Eccl. 12:1?

4. Who is he talking to in Eccl. 12:6-8?

We've discussed before how God created us so that we would REACH for Him (Acts 17:27). THIS is what you were made for! Men AND women were created to bring glory to God.

So – you are a female created to glorify God. How does He want you to do that, exactly?

Read 1 Timothy 2:8-15

5. What are the women to do in "like manner" to the men lifting up "holy hands" in 1 Tim. 2:8-9?

6.These things are proper for whom? (verse 10)

7. Look up the Greek word, and its definition, for "silence" in verses 11-12.

8. Explain what you think 1 Timothy 2:15 means.

The picture we've been given here is of a woman who dresses in a way that REFLECTS the meek and quiet spirit that she has INSIDE. Wait – where have we heard that before?

1 Peter 3:1-6 begins with the words "Wives, likewise…" This means that this section is connected to the section that came before. So let's look at what came before.

9. What does 1 Peter 2:11-12 say honorable conduct will do?

10. Who is to submit in 1 Peter 2:13?

    To whom are they to submit? (verses 14-17)

11. Who is to submit in 1 Peter 2:18?

    To whom are they to submit?

12. Why were we "called" to do this? (verse 21)

So that brings us back to 1 Peter 3:1-6. We've talked about this several times now. Let's look at just a few things now.

13. Look up the Greek word and definition for "submissive" in 1 Peter 3:1.

Understand that submission is not about our value, it is about our FUNCTION. What role we play in the grand scheme God has for mankind.

14. What may teach a husband to be a Christian? (verses 1-2)

We've already covered how the hidden person of the heart is to be our focus. Our beauty begins there. If you are not beautiful inside, you will not be beautiful outside. Focus on this aspect of your beauty and you will shine!

Let's go back to our Study Builder verse.

15. Write 1 Timothy 4:12 here.

Do you remember 2 Peter 1:5-9? Let's look at it again.

Read 2 Peter 1:5-9.

16. List the items to be "added" that are in these verses.
    1.
    2.
    3.
    4.
    5.
    6.
    7.
    8.

17. To what are you to add these things? (v.5)

18. How are you to add these things? (v.5)

19. Why should we add these things? (v.8)

20. If you don't add these things what are you? (v.9)

There's that RECIPE God gave for living a life that will take you into the kingdom of our Lord and Savior Jesus Christ! (verse 11)

So, what do you believe you need to know to be a wife and mother? Do you realize that God says that you need to be TAUGHT how to do these jobs? Just as a child won't do the right thing unless you teach him (Prov. 22:15), so too a young woman must be taught how to do as she should as woman, wife, and mother. Fortunately, again, God has covered EVERYTHING. I just think that's fabulous!

Read Titus 2:3-5.

21. Describe an older woman from these verses.

22. The older woman is to teach the young woman to:

    a.   b.

    c.   d.

    e.   f.

    g.

23. Why do they teach these things? (verse 5)

24. Do a WORD STUDY on the things you listed in question 22. Look up the word to define it, then look up other verses that use the same word to further help you to understand what it means.

To be a woman is a hard job! Paul says in 1 Corinthians 7:32-35 that being unmarried and focusing on obeying the Lord is concern enough, and it is a blessing to be able to focus only on serving Him. Being married is a good thing as well, but it forces one to care about worldly things in addition to spiritual things. The glorious thing is that God has given each of us what we need to get through it all (1 Peter 1:3)! He's even created a relationship for you to have a natural teacher of these things, your mother and the older women in your life! So, listen to them, learn from them, and then when YOU are the older woman TEACH them to the younger women. This guarantees generations of people who will be seeking after the Lord (Matthew 28:20)!

This time of your life, whatever season you are in, is a blessed event. Cherish it, but guard it well!

Many blessings,

Mrs. Angela Legg

Study Builders

Use this page to note all the verses from the lesson into one or more of the categories.

In Manner of Life In Purity	In Word
In Love	In Faith

Additional Notes:

Bonus Lesson

Warnings from Dinah, Tamar, Tamar

These lessons, I personally believe, are best taught one on one between mother and daughter or older woman and younger woman, especially for a younger age group. God's word is always proper and right, but should be considered for the audience (Is. 28:10; 1 Pet. 2:2; Heb. 5:12, 13). I give you this lesson to teach at your discretion. I pray that it may be beneficial.

Scripture References: Gen. 30:21; Gen. 34; Gen. 38; 1 Chron. 2:4; Mt. 1:3; 2 Sam. 13; 1 Chron. 3:9

<u>Dinah</u>

1. Who were Dinah's parents? (Genesis 30:20, 21; 34:1)

2. Where did Dinah go in Genesis 34:1?

3. Did Dinah's family see this as something that was all right, they just would have preferred if Shechem had married her first? (Gen. 34:7)

What Shechem did, could not be undone. One lesson that can be learned here is one kind of trouble often leads to another. God set an order to things 'in the beginning" (Matthew 19:4-6). When we go against that order, it IS going to bring trouble.

<u>Tamar</u>

4. Who was Tamar? (Genesis 38:6)

5. In Genesis 38:14, Tamar took off her _____ _____.

6. She put on clothes that made Judah think she was a _____. (Genesis 38:14-15)

This story shows that clothes identify us to others. Tamar's choices were deliberate. We must each be deliberate to AVOID what she was seeking to look like. The world likes to tell us that what we wear doesn't give an invitation to people to stare or think things they shouldn't be thinking. The world is WRONG. 1 Timothy 2:9 says, "in like manner also, that the women adorn themselves in modest apparel, with propriety and moderation…" If I'm supposed to know what MODEST apparel is, then it follows that I will know what IMMODEST apparel is! The people looking at you have to take care of what they look at and what they think – you have to help by not putting a stumbling block in their way (Romans 14:13; Matthew 18:6)

Tamar

7. Who was Tamar? (2 Sam. 13:1; 1 Chron. 3:1-9)

8. How is Jonadab described in 2 Samuel 13:3?

9. What kind of clothes did Tamar have on? (2 Sam. 13:18)

10. What did Absalom do to Amnon because of what Amnon did to Tamar? (2 Sam. 13:32)

This story teaches us that sometimes things happen to us even when we do everything we can to keep it from happening. When people want to do bad things, often they will. Tamar did what she could to make Amnon do what was right. He would not hear her. God's word in the Old Law would not hold her accountable for this. She did what she could, but unfortunately, she also had to live with the results. When there is sin in the world, we all will suffer because of it. This is what makes us YEARN for HEAVEN. Jesus certainly understands what Tamar went through – He knows all about people choosing to do the wrong things even though you've reminded them of what is right! We need to learn that Jesus can get us through anything (Phil. 4:13). Absalom didn't do right in murdering his brother, God had laws in place that would have dealt with Amnon – but David didn't enforce them, and Absalom took matters into his own hands. Once again, we see that one wrong just leads to another wrong.

So, pay attention to your surroundings.

Be careful of the friends you choose – are they going to lead you to do what is right?

You do the best that you can do, and let God take care of the rest,

We all are going to sin (Romans 3:23), but the Lord will forgive if we repent and obey His word.

Read Psalm 51:10-11

It is said that this Psalm was written by David after he realized all his sins in taking Bathsheba for his own. What does he ask the Lord to do in verse 10?

David had sinned, would God have been right to turn away from David?

Instead, David asks what in verse 11?

Write a prayer that asks God to help you be pure in heart.

Study Builders

Use this page to note all the verses from the lesson into one or more of the categories.

In Manner of Life In Purity	In Word
In Love	In Faith

Additional Notes:

APPENDIX

Teacher's Notes for Song of Solomon

I am including with each lesson what I understand each section of speaking to be talking about. *****

The Song of Solomon is a much-contested book of the Bible. There are several different concepts applied to the book. This is covered more in depth in True Love vs Sensuality.

My understanding is that of a story of Solomon the King, the Shulammite shepherdess/vinedresser, and the Shepherd who is her Beloved. The largest motivator for my taking this position is that I believe the book must uphold God's teachings on marriage (Gen.2:18-24; 1 Cor.7:1-11; Eph. 5:22-33). The teaching in this book must be consistent with other Biblical teaching about marriage and the love that is found in that relationship.

Therefore, I cannot understand the book to be teaching of Solomon having a righteous, lovely, intimate – and thereby to be imitated – marriage while also having "sixty queens", "eighty concubines", and "virgins without number" (S of S 6:8). Even giving allowances for the language of poetry there is no other way to take the original Hebrew words in this verse for anything other than women of Solomon's court. Jesus said, "Have you not read that He who created them from the beginning made them male and female, and said, 'For this reason a man shall leave his father and mother and be joined to his wife, and the two shall become one flesh'?" (Matthew 19:4-5).

In Deuteronomy 17:17, God lays out the behavior He will demand of the King that Israel will demand to have later, "He shall not multiply wives for himself, or else his heart will turn away;". God would not tell us it was wrong for the King to have multiple wives then show us how to have a godly marriage within the sin of having multiple wives. There are loving relationships found in marriages where the man had multiple wives (Jacob and Rachel, Elkanah and Hannah) but these do not uphold the ideal that God set forth in Genesis 2:18-24, and show the problems that come about when God's ideal is not upheld.

Song of Solomon, to be a song of true love and marriage at its best, cannot hold to the sins of Solomon AND uphold one of his marriages as God ordained, in my opinion. To do so, one must forcibly ignore other scripture references and hold Song of Solomon separate and apart – something for which Christians should not hold tolerance for in regards to proper study of Scripture. It's either ALL God's word AND is harmonious – or it is NOT God's word. It cannot be God's word and have deliberate conflicts of teaching and ideals.

I hope to give you my thoughts in hopes that it will aid you in using the material as I have included it in To Be a Handmaid of the Lord. I could find two of the commentaries that are referred to by the teacher whose outline I loosely follow for this study. I was able to read through those commentaries. I was loaned a third that was not in the original list on the outline.

Having read these commentaries, having studied Song of Solomon, and having compared the poetry in it to other places that use similar language in scripture, I find no reason for the text to be considered highly sexual. Even where there is double meaning that is obvious, it is not written in any way that is greatly explicit. The book talks about physical intimacy in the frame of being rightly anticipated as something that comes within marriage. The knowledge that human bodies are made for physical pleasure is embraced, references that are crude show the difference between the man who has the best interests of his woman at heart and the man who does not. I pray that you will not find anything immodest in the way I refer to things. These things would be immodest if spoken of outside of the sanctity of marriage or in terms that degraded the intimacy to nothing more than physical pleasure alone. There is balance in these things, and I believe this book teaches that balance.

Further explanation and examples can be found in the essay "True Love vs Sensuality" that follows these notes.

General Thoughts on the Setting and Circumstances of Song of Solomon

In the lessons, I have typed my understanding of the verse to the right of the verse. If a statement is obvious in its meaning, I make no comment.

Part 1 of the play takes place in the "Royal Tents in Issachar".

The "royal tents" is understood from S of S 1:4 and 1:12. The idea that the story begins in Issachar comes from S of S 7:13, where the daughters of Jerusalem refer to the woman as "Shulamite". This is thought, by several commentaries, to refer to the city of Sunem or Shunem, which was in the lands given to Issachar (Joshua 19:18; 1 Kings 1:3; 2 Kings 4:8). It is seen also as Shulem, Suwlam, and Solam in various writings. Here is a map that indicates where Shunem of Issachar was located.

As a scene setting – I visualize a young woman from the country who has been chosen to be a woman in King Solomon's harem of women. (This was done to Esther by the King of Persia, done for David with Abishag (1 Kings 1), and foretold by God that Israel's kings would take the women of the land for his servants (Deut. 17:14-17; 1 Sam. 8:10-18), so a country girl who is out of her element in the royal household would not be an impossible happening. This young woman already has a young man who has expressed interest in her (S of S 2:10-14) and he is a shepherd (S of S 1:7). She is in the tents of King Solomon. Royal activity goes on around her, even includes her, but her mind keeps going back home to what she knows. This is where we find her as the story begins.

Song of Solomon:

True Love vs Sensuality

I am not a Bible scholar, but I do find it interesting that such a small book causes such disagreement between those who claim to be Bible scholars.

There are several prominent theories as to what the book is about. The commentaries that you find, for the most part, take two points of view: the book is about Solomon and one of his wives and the beautiful love story they lived; or the book is a general love theme that is an allegory for Christ and the Church. Both points of view often take a highly-sexualized interpretation of the poetry in which the song is written. The thing that is most interesting, regarding the scholars' interpretations, is that when you read their commentaries, there is no real explanation for WHY the book must be one or the other. Those things come about in their discussions of their own opinions. They do not go to scripture to attempt to explain why God would create one book that reflects the church in such a highly human and sexual way, or why God would create a book that exults a marriage that is one of many to a King when He spends a great deal of His word condemning the act of having multiple marriages and sexual relations outside of the one man/one woman relationship.

I am a simple woman. I long only to study God's word so that I may garner the understanding that He has promised (Eph. 5:17; Ps. 111:10; Jn.7:17; 1 Thess. 4:1-2) and that which Solomon himself recognized he could only get from God (1 Kings 3:9). I know that God has put The Song of Solomon in the Bible for each of us to learn something (Rom. 15:4) and that teaching will harmonize with all of God's other teachings (Acts 15:15; 1 John 5:8; Matt. 5:17; 1 Kings 8:56).

Those very understandings begin the approach I make when studying The Song of Solomon. I expressed in my Notes on Song of Solomon my belief that this book is a story of a young woman, the Shulamite (S of S 6:13) making a choice between the Shepherd/Beloved who is back home (S of S 2:16-17) and Solomon the king who has brought her to be one of his many women (S of S 1:4; 6:8).

I believe that Solomon could have written a book in which he does not come out the winner. It would not be the first time the wisest man (2 Chron. 1:8-13; 2 Chron. 9:22-24) other than Jesus penned words that he, himself, did not follow (Prov. 5:15-23; Eccl. 12:9-13). Solomon taught much on seeking the wisdom of God and not straying from it (Prov. 1:8-10, 15; 2:1-6; 3:1-12), but he allowed himself to be drawn away by the many foreign women he married against the instructions of the Lord (Deut. 17:14-20; 1 Kings 11:1-10; Neh. 13:26).

I also believe that someone else could have written this story to demonstrate the great choice the woman makes and God directed him to use Solomon as the ultimate example of worldliness and luxury. We aren't told who wrote the book – it's simply called the Song of Songs. It's an ultimate song of love, and it mentions Solomon, but beyond that, the scholars agree, we do not know with certainty the author of the book.

As an exercise in studying what the book actually says, instead of what men think it might say, please consider these questions:

1. How does one harmonize Jesus' teachings in Matthew 19:4-9, Moses' understanding in Genesis 2:24, and the teachings of Paul in 1 Corinthians 7:1-5 and Ephesians 5:22-33 with the idea that Solomon's bringing this young woman into his harem (Song of Solomon 6:8-9) is righteous with God?

2. If Solomon is the "Beloved" the Shulamite longs for:

   a. Why does she wear a reminder of him while in his presence? (Song of Solomon 1:12-14)

   b. Why, when she is in Solomon's royal tents (Song of Solomon 1:4), does she refer to their house as being a natural one (trees) (Song of Solomon 1:16-17)?

   c. Why do the "daughters of Jerusalem", who are likely the women of Solomon's court which would include wives and concubines, ask for a description of the Beloved (Song of Solomon 5:9)?

   d. Why does the Shulamite tell the daughters of Jerusalem to go find "my beloved" (Song of Solomon 5:8) if she is married to him and dwells with him?

   e. Why, after the Shulamite describes her beloved, do these women long to go find him (Song of Solomon 6:1) if he is the same man to whom they have access?

   f. Why does the Shulamite continually describe Solomon (if he is the Beloved) as a shepherd working out in the mountains (Song of Solomon 1:7; 2:8-9, 16-17; 6:2-3)? There is no Bible reference to Solomon being associated with shepherding. He was born far into David's kingship and would not have been brought up in a country way of life. There is also no record of Solomon going and making a home in the countryside any of his wives was from. Why assume she describes this regal king in this way?

g. Compare Song of Solomon 4:1-5, 7 with Song of Solomon 6:4-9. Think about the comparisons made. Solomon speaks of "city" type things here; chariots, armies, towers, etc. Now look at Song of Solomon 4:8-15. This description of the Shulamite is made in "country" terms; single strand of necklace, wine, oils, honey, milk, etc. If the same person is speaking, why the switch in focus and choice of words?

h. Why does Solomon call the Shulamite "my darling" ("my love" in other translations) in S of S 4:1, 7 and 6:4 which is agreed by scholars is a general term that infers that he doesn't know her well, yet (if Solomon is the beloved) call her "my bride", "my sister", in 4:8-12, which implies that she is engaged to him, not yet married, and they know one another so well he considers her as his "sister"?

i. The conversation flows logically from beginning to end – warm thoughts of the Beloved, praises for the Shulamite, anticipation for the coming benefits of marriage – if this is a story of a man and woman already married, why does the Shulamite worry that she has lost her beloved by being indecisive (S of S 5:2-7)?

j. Again, with the flow of conversation, why the need for a warning of not allowing jealousy to come between them (S of S 8:6-7)? If the story is of a happy couple long married enjoying one another completely, the insertion of jealousy without preamble is awkward and does not fit the tone of the rest of the story.

k. Why does the Shulamite fear not being able to find a husband she already has (if Solomon is the Beloved) (S of S 3:1-4)?

There is another aspect of the general beliefs of the religious community that I would like to address – the need to interpret every reference to fruit and flowers as something graphically sexual. Personally, I believe that the lengths some go to be graphic about these scriptures is nothing more than a lustful desire to discuss things that are private in a public setting while claiming God's divine plan to do so.

My understanding of these references is obvious. These things represent pleasant things that are shared between these people, or anticipate to be shared. But to make it in graphic, specific action is to take it beyond the context, the intent of the original Hebrew, and the tone of scripture in general.

I do have a thought process for why I believe this. God did not see fit to describe in intimate detail all the normal, instinctual functions of human life. From the beginning,

He allowed for some things to just be understood because it was mankind reading about mankind.

In Genesis 4:1 the NASB says, "Now the man had relations with his wife Eve"; the KJV says "And Adam knew his wife Eve"; it is only the New Living Translation and New International Version which step forward to say "sexual relations" or "made love to". In all other translations, it is understood what is meant by "Adam knew his wife". No explanation or details are necessary.

Again, in Genesis 4:17, "Cain had relations with his wife".

Note Genesis 9:21, 22 "He drank of the wine and became drunk, and uncovered himself inside his tent. Ham, the father of Canaan, saw the nakedness of his father, and told his two brothers outside." God chooses not to give us details – we get the point without discussion.

When we read the account in Genesis 19:1-11, most people are mortified at the obvious vulgarity of the men of Sodom. Again, the translators of most Bibles use "know them" or "relations with them" to tell us what these evil men wanted to do. It is only in two modern Bibles, the New Living Translation and New International Version that go to the more blunt "have sex with them". Later in the chapter, 19:32, we understand what Lot's oldest daughter means by "let us lie with him". God didn't see fit to get explicit – I believe there's no need for us to go further than He does!

Proverbs 5:15-23 is a pointed scripture where Solomon teaches that married men should keep themselves at home with their wives. He uses poetic language to avoid being immodest, in my opinion. He certainly could say these things straight out, for example, God didn't use poetic language in Genesis 38:9. Solomon makes the point of keeping your sexual activity at home with your spouse in terms that can be spoken without being improper. It also lends to the idea that intimacy is more than just a physical need being met – it is connected with life, a connection between two people that emotes emotions, and something precious to be protected. All in the words he chooses to use instead of the blunt obvious. It is again, only a modern translation that felt the need to be more explicit in the translation (New Living Translation says "share your love only with your wife"). This isn't translating, it's explaining. The New Living Translation is wording the intent instead of translating the actual Hebrew words into the English word that means the same. God allows for men to understand the nature of human sexual relations. When He is being obvious about something particular, but using a gentle allusion to it rather than stating it, this is obvious.

There are a few references in Song of Solomon that are obviously very blunt sexual references masked in slightly more gentle words – Song of Solomon 7:7-9 "Your stature is like a palm tree, and your breasts are like its clusters. I said, 'I will climb the palm tree, I will take hold of its fruit stalks.' Oh, may your breasts be like clusters of the vine, and the fragrance of your breath like apples, and your mouth like the best wine!" There is no other rendering than Solomon wants to use her body for sexual pleasure. But the context is a build up to this very blatant statement that goes against the modesty of all previous comments. Solomon is pushing this young woman, he's following the very physical speech of his other women and hoping that the Shulamite is being flattered by it all. He declares boldly that he sees her as something to be grabbed and taken physically.

The stark contrast is how the Beloved describes the Shulamite back in chapter 4. In verse 11 it says, "Your lips, my bride, drip honey; Honey and milk are under your tongue, and the fragrance of your garments is like the fragrance of Lebanon." Simply put – good things come from your mouth and your clothes smell good. Milk and honey are often used in scripture to refer to things that are simply beneficial.

> The land of Canaan is one in Numbers 13:27, "Thus they told him, and said, 'We went in to the land where you sent us; and it certainly does flow with milk and honey, and this is its fruit.'"

"Milk and honey" was an obvious reference to a land that has an abundance of water, grass, plants, trees, flowers, etc. Milk and honey are produced by having access to these things.

> Psalm 19:10 refers to God's judgments as "sweeter than honey and the drippings of the honeycomb". God's judgments are plentiful and beneficial for us.

> In Proverb 5:2 we are given a context that involves sexual immorality, but even in this context the honey of her lips is nothing more than the words she speaks because it is explained as, "for the lips of an adulteress drip honey and smoother than oil is her speech;" – the honey has to do with this evil woman using words the young man will like to hear. Nothing more.

> Nowhere else in scripture are the words "milk" or "honey" used to refer to anything other than milk or honey, or to refer to their known qualities, such as sweetness. Why assume Song of Solomon means something highly sexualized? Going back to Song of Solomon 4:11, and taking everything else the Bible says about "honey" – the beloved says of the Shulamite that she speaks kind and beneficial words and that she and her clothes are clean and smell of the environment in which she spends her time – trees and flowers. Is there an implication that the Beloved likes this about her? Absolutely! He is describing all the good things about her – what makes her beautiful to him.

A comparable verse would be Proverbs 31:26, "She opens her mouth in wisdom, and the teaching of kindness is on her tongue."

References to the Shulamite being a garden do have double meaning, but they do so without being blunt and immodest, hence the garden reference. She is a beautiful woman, full of beautiful things. She is pleasant and he expects to enjoy his time with her – intimacy is implied, but it's not the only implication, he will enjoy his LIFE with this woman. Song of Solomon 4:12 says that she is "a spring sealed up". If you take what we learned from Proverbs 5:15ff and apply it here – she is keeping her sexual self to herself until she is married to him. She heeds the warning of Solomon in Proverbs! These are people who have a healthy understanding of what God made their bodies to do, but they are anticipating it rightly within the bounds of marriage. The scriptures are not describing their acts of intimacy in detail otherwise not used in the Bible! To make it so, is to make the verses focus on the physical only. In my estimation, Song of Solomon glorifies the man and woman who appreciate the physical, spiritual, and emotional aspects of one another. Those who focus on the physical only, i.e. Solomon and his women, are the ones out of balance.

When the Shulamite says "Awake, O north wind, and come wind of the south; Make my garden breathe out fragrance, let its spices be wafted abroad. May my beloved come into his garden and eat its choice fruits!" (S of S 4:16), she's saying, "let me be all that he sees in me. Let me be the beneficial, inviting, enjoyable mate that he desires." It doesn't have to be explained in graphic detail. It can be said in sweet simplicity, and understood on an intimate level without making it grotesque.

References to feeding flocks among the lilies are simply that – a shepherd from the valleys in the land of Issachar finding good sources of food for his sheep. He doesn't just find scruff, he finds choice feed for his sheep. She knows he does his job well and takes care of those in his charge. She appreciates this in him. (Song of Solomon 1:7; 2:16-17; 6:2-3)

If you read the book of Song of Solomon through from beginning to end, you will find that the very time when the couple are coming to their wedding and life together the tone of the story changes to one of describing a life together that is anticipated rather than individuals who have already been connected for some time. The last thing said is the Beloved's call to the Shulamite, "My friends are waiting to hear you say it. Let me hear you." She responds with, "Let's hurry and make a life full of the blessings we've promised each other!" (Song of Solomon 8:13-14).

All the questions I listed, none of the commentaries attempted to answer. The commentaries simply dismiss the possibility of a simple story of a country girl choosing between the city life with a King and the country life with a shepherd. Most of them take obscure references to possible poetry written at the time of Song of Solomon (which is greatly debated as well) and derive possible meanings for the words they then decide must mean sexual acts.

Please do not misunderstand me, I do believe that Song of Solomon teaches that any young person is right to realize that her body is made to be pleasing to her spouse. She is right to anticipate the pleasures that come with the physical intimacy reserved for the married couple. I just do not believe that God makes this point by detailing sexual positions like the Kama Sutra. One study of Song of Solomon puts forth this very idea – the author attempts to keep it chaste and warns that the study is only for those getting ready to enter marriage or who are already married – but still, the assumptions of what God is telling in the scriptures borders on pornographic. I had one friend tell me that she had stayed away from studying Song of Solomon because one time a preacher spoke of the book in such lascivious ways that she was embarrassed sitting in the room listening to him, and disgusted that anything that graphic would be in God's word. His handling of God's word made her afraid to even approach it because he had attached Song of Solomon to the overly sexed rather than the properly sensual. It was obvious that he was extracting pleasure from having the blatant discussion. Shame!

I believe that the subtly of Song of Solomon allows this book to be taught to any age group that has entered puberty. (I do not teach David and Bathsheba or the rape of Tamar by Amnon to 7 and 8 year olds, I certainly would not teach Song of Solomon to them.) You just handle the awkward phrases differently with each type of group. You don't get very specific with the very innocent. There is no reason, in my opinion, to encourage their thinking on these things at an early age. Simply teach about the desire for marriage, the desire to be close, and the rightness of finding the opposite sex attractive and pleasing. With the older groups, especially those near marrying age, you can be a bit more specific – but even this can be summed up in chaste terms. Something like "The Shulamite knows her body is a garden of good fruit. She hopes that she will be pleasing to him", generally covers it. No need to get into HOW she pleases him. The text doesn't even deal with this – it is only alluded to. No reason we cannot follow the example.

I truly do not want my opinion to be taken for gospel on this study. I believe that there is enough question about Song of Solomon's origins that to make a stand about the point of view one way or the other is not a matter of fellowship. But I will say that I believe, and my questions show my thought process, that it is foolish to spend a great deal of time studying Song of Solomon without comparing it fully to the rest of the Bible. It is a unique book, but not so much so that we cannot have confidence in its teaching. Taking stands that make these sexualized references as being about Christ and the Church all the while stating that the relationship between them is a spiritual one, not a physical one – just seems counterintuitive, but again, this is my opinion. I teach this book the way I have stated because it is the best way I can find to teach it and not be in contradiction with other scripture. If you find anything in your study that shows that I am in error, you would be my friend to point this out to me. I offer it only for you to take as a consideration and an understanding of how the material in "To Be a Handmaid of the Lord" is written.

Diligently,

Angela Legg

Made in the USA
San Bernardino, CA
10 April 2017